*Includes authentic video
from the BBC*

British News Update 2

Timothy Knowles   Mayumi Tamura

Minne Tanaka   Mihoko Nakamura

KINSEIDO

Kinseido Publishing Co., Ltd.
3-21 Kanda Jimbo-cho, Chiyoda-ku,
Tokyo 101-0051, Japan

First published 2020 by Kinseido Publishing Co., Ltd.

News clips ©BBC 2019.
Images ©BBC 2019.
Cover images ©BBC 2019.

This edition produced under licence by Kinseido Publishing Co., Ltd. 2020.

BBCニュース ホームページ：www.bbc.com/news

Introduction

The British Broadcasting Corporation (BBC) is internationally famous for the quality and impartiality of its news items. BBC reporters also strive to make the news both interesting and as easy to understand as possible. In this book we have chosen 15 items that we think would be of particular interest. Most are about Britain, as you might expect, but many of the issues covered, such as health, education, and the environment are generally familiar to Japanese learners. There are also some important international issues, and topics that are included because they give a fascinating insight into a different culture.

It is hoped that the items will be motivating, and that students will be eager to watch and listen because they are interested in what they are discovering. New and important items of vocabulary are introduced, and the notes (in Japanese) will explain any interesting and important points of grammar and usage of English. However, perhaps the most important purpose of this book is that the learners should be able to engage in the subject matter, and then discuss it and research it together. With this in mind, we have developed discussion questions that would encourage them to relate these new discoveries with what is already familiar to them in Japan.

Finally, it is important to keep up with the technology that is now available to students. Therefore, videos are now easily accessible online. This will make it easy for students to study by themselves out of class.

We hope you enjoy the book and the videos.

はじめに

　本書は、実際に放送された BBC（英国放送協会）のニュースを教材として、ニュースキャスターや街頭インタヴューを受ける native speaker が自然に話す英語に触れることで、学習者のリスニング力や語彙力といった英語力を伸ばすことを目的としています。同時に、イギリスや世界で起こっている出来事やその背景となる社会や文化についても学べるように工夫されています。

　扱うトピックは、政治、経済、環境など多岐にわたるものとし、できるだけ up to date でありつつも、普遍的なものを選びました。学習する皆様の興味関心の幅を広げ、ご希望にお応えすることができれば幸いです。

　本シリーズは昨年よりタイトルを一新し、新たなスタートを切りました。ただし、内容は前シリーズを引き継いでおります。ユニット内のコラムは、イギリス文化についての面白い情報を増やして充実を図り、Questions も最初の Setting the Scene に始まり、Follow Up にいたるまで、各ユニットで取り上げるニュースを順序良く掘り下げて理解が深まるように配慮しました。

　本書を通じて、伝統と革新が共存する多民族国家イギリスが、4 つの地域の独自性を保ちつつ、総体としてのイギリスらしさ（“Britishness”）を模索する今の姿を見ていただけると思います。現在のイギリスは、EU からの離脱やスコットランドの独立などの多くの問題を抱えており、日本や世界に与える影響を考慮すると、今後もその動きから目が離せません。

　このテキストを使って学習する皆様が、イギリスや世界の状勢に興味をもち、さらには、自分から英語ニュースに触れたり、英語で意見を述べたりと、ますます学習の場が広がっていきますことを、執筆者一同願っております。

　最後になりましたが、本書の作成にあたり、BBC ニュースを教材として使うことを許可して下さいました BBC と、編集に際してご尽力いただきました金星堂の皆様に、この場をお借りして、心より感謝申し上げます。

本書の使い方

テキストの特徴

　普段の生活の中で、ニュースの英語に触れる機会はあまりないかもしれません。本テキストは、初めて英語でニュースを観る場合でも無理なく取り組めるよう、多種多様なアクティビティを用意しています。単語のチェックや内容確認、穴埋め、要約、ディスカッションを通して、段階を踏みながらニュースを理解できるような作りになっているので、達成感を感じることができるでしょう。

Starting Off

1.　Setting the Scene

　実際にニュースを観る前に、ニュースで扱われるトピックについて考えるためのセクションです。トピックについての学習を始めるにあたり、身近な問題としてトピックを捉えられるような問題を用意しました。ここで先にニュースに関する情報を整理しておけば、実際にニュースを観る際に理解が容易になります。ニュースで使われている単語や語句、または重要な概念をここで予習しておきましょう。

2.　Building Language

　ニュースの中で使われる重要単語を学びます。単に日本語の訳語を覚えるのではなく、英語での定義を通して、また同義語を覚えながら、単語の持つ意味を英語で理解することを目指します。また、これらの単語はディスカッションを行うときにもおそらく頻繁に使うことになる単語ですし、ニュースの核となる単語ですので、発音もしっかりと確認することが重要です。

Watching the News

3.　Understanding Check 1

　実際にニュースの中身を詳しく見ていく前に、どんな意見が交わされているのかを確認します。ここで具体的にニュースのイメージをつかむことが大事です。全体像を簡単にでも把握することで、ニュース理解の大きな助けとなります。

4.　Understanding Check 2

　ニュースに関する問題を解くことで、どれだけニュースを理解できたか確認することができます。間違えた箇所に関しては、なぜ間違えたのかをしっかりと分析し、内容を正確に把握しましょう。Filling Gapsのアクティビティﾞを行ってからUnderstanding Check 2に取り組むのも効果的かもしれません。

5.　Filling Gaps

　ニュースの中で重要な意味を持つ単語を聞き取ります。何度も繰り返し聞き、正しい発音を意識します。それと同時に、単語を正しく書き取ることで、耳と手との両方の動きを通して重要単語を習得することを目指します。もし時間に余裕があれば、穴埋めの単語を実際に発音し、耳と手に加え口も使って覚えると効果的です。

Moving On
6.　Making a Summary

　この箇所は、これまで観てきたニュースをまとめる部分でもあり、かつFollow Upに至る前の準備の段階でもあります。しっかりと内容を理解しているか、このアクティビティを通して確認しましょう。また、Building Languageで出てきた単語を再度使っているため、単語の習熟の確認ができるようになっています。

7.　Follow Up

　ニュースと関連したトピックをいくつか挙げてあります。ニュースで得た知識、また単語を活かして話し合いを行うためのセクションです。トピックには、その場で話し合えるものと各自調べてから発表し合うもの、両方が含まれています。そのニュースに関してだけでなく、今後似たような話題に接したときにも意見を述べることができるよう、このアクティビティで仕上げを行います。

Background Information

　ニュースでは、必ずしもすべての事柄が説明されているとは限りません。ニュースの核となる事柄で、かつニュースの中ではあまり詳しく説明されていないことに関して、このセクションでは補足しています。ニュースをより深く理解するのにも役立ちますし、Follow Upでの話し合いの際にも使えるかもしれません。

Behind the Scenes

　ニュースに関連することではありますが、Background Informationとは異なりここではニュースの核となることではなく、話題が広がる知識、教養が深まる知識を取り上げました。肩の力を抜き、楽しんで読めるような内容になっています。

・各ユニットで取り上げたニュース映像はオンラインで視聴することができます。詳しくは巻末を参照ください。

・テキスト準拠のAudio CDには、各ユニットのニュース音声と、ニュースを学習用に聞き取りやすく吹き替えた音声、Making a Summaryを収録しています。

Contents

Map of The United Kingdom

正式名称は **The United Kingdom of Great Britain and Northern Ireland**（グレートブリテン及び北アイルランド連合王国）。**England**（イングランド）、**Wales**（ウェールズ）、**Scotland**（スコットランド）、**Northern Ireland**（北アイルランド）の 4 国から成る連合国家です（**2020** 年現在）。

※（　）は本テキストでその地名、場所が登場するユニットを表します

Unit 1

A Coffee Shop in a Phone Box

ロンドンといえば、二階建てバス、黒いタクシーに、赤い電話ボックス。しかし、携帯電話の普及と共に、公衆電話が激減しました。使われなくなった電話ボックスの活用を巡って、一騒動ありました。ニュースを見てみましょう。

▶ Starting Off

1 Setting the Scene

▌ What do you think?

1. Do you like to drink coffee when you are out? Describe an interesting or strange coffee shop that you know.
2. If you start selling coffee in Japan, do you think you need a licence? What rules do you think there might be?
3. Before most people had mobile phones, there used to be lots of phone boxes in the streets. What has happened to these phone boxes? Are they still there?

2 Building Language

▌ For each word (1-6), find two synonyms (a-l).

1. stir	[/]	**a.** publish	**g.** best	
2. squeeze	[/]	**b.** uproar	**h.** problem	
3. submit	[/]	**c.** hand in	**i.** deliver	
4. prime	[/]	**d.** excellent	**j.** fuss	
5. issue (as noun)	[/]	**e.** crowd	**k.** controversy	
6. issue (as verb)	[/]	**f.** crush	**l.** propose	

③ Understanding Check 1

▍ Read the quotes, then watch the news and match them to the right people.

1. No problem whatsoever selling the coffee . . .   [   ]

2. But we have seen creative ways of giving them a new lease of life. [   ]

3. I think it's absolutely brilliant. [   ]

4. Some might say that the idea is lovely . . .   [   ]

④ Understanding Check 2

▍ Which is the best answer?

1. Which of the following possible uses of a phone box was <u>not</u> mentioned?
   a. a shoe repair shop
   b. a mobile phone repair shop
   c. a café
   d. a lending library

2. Which <u>two</u> of the following were mentioned as being good points of the phone box café?
   a. The coffee is delicious.
   b. It looks lovely.
   c. You can make telephone calls while you drink coffee.
   d. It's a good place for people to meet and talk together.
   e. It's close to the train station.
   f. The coffee is cheap.

3. How much was the café owner fined altogether?
   a. £150
   b. £300
   c. £450
   d. £600

▌What do you remember?

4. Why is the café against the law?

---

5. Why does the café owner feel that the council's rules are ridiculous?

---

6. What has the café owner applied for?

●●Background Information●●

　今回のニュースは、イギリス全土で使われなくなった赤電話ボックス（the red phone box）が様々に改造され、利用されているという話題でした。その背景には、携帯電話の普及で電話ボックスによる通話が過去10年間で90％減少し、電話ボックスの3分の1が全く使用されていない、という状況があります。しかし、2015年に行われた投票により、第2位のダブルデッカー・バス、第3位のユニオンジャック旗を抑えて「イギリス史上最高のデザイン」の第1位に選ばれるなど、赤電話ボックスはイギリス国民にとってなおも愛着のあるものになっています。

　電話ボックスの原型は1920年にコンクリートで作られましたが、1924年にサー・ジャイルズ・ギルバート・スコット（Sir Giles Gilbert Scott, 1880-1960）がデザイン・コンテストで優勝し、K2モデルが作成されました。さらに、1935年、ジョージ5世（King George V, 1865-1936）の即位25周年（the Silver Jubilee）を祝って新しい電話ボックスがスコットに委託され、お馴染みのK6モデルが誕生しました。

　このように国民に愛された電話ボックスを撤去するのは忍びないということで、ブリティッシュ・テレコム（BT: British Telecom）は2012年から「電話ボックスを活用しよう計画（the Adopt a Kiosk scheme）」を開始し、1ポンドという金額で、多くの地域共同体に電話ボックスを販売しています。その結果、4,000を超える赤電話ボックスがアート・ギャラリー、心臓除細動器の収納場所、インフォメーション・センター、展示場などに再利用され、人々に喜ばれています。

　ところが、ニュースに登場した「レッド・コーヒー・ボックス店（Red Coffee Box）」は、露天営業許可（street trading licence）を巡り、ハウンズロウの地方議会と対立することになりました。議会は、メフメット氏がテーブルと椅子を置いて営業するなら許可が必要であるとし、メフメット氏はこれを申請しましたが、地域住民や事業者の反対、3度の罰金を払っていないことなどを理由に、結局、申請は却下されてしまいました。

参考：https://www.bbc.com/news/magazine-32315904
　　　https://www.bbc.com/news/uk-england-36148287
　　　http://www.chiswickw4.com/default.asp?section＝info&page＝redboxcoffee003.htm

Filling Gaps | **News Story** ⊙ CD1-02 [Original] ⊙ CD1-03 [Voiced]

Watch the news, then fill the gaps in the text.

Newsreader: Now, London's red phone boxes, no longer in use, but still a landmark. But we have seen creative ways of giving them a new lease of life. This one, (¹   ) between Harrods and Harvey Nichols, is now used as a shop to repair mobile phones. Er, and this, has become a local lending library. The clever conversions have generally been welcomed. But the latest one is causing a bit of a (²   ), as Emma North explains.

Emma North: For the people who work, and drink, at this phone box-turned-café in Turnham Green, it's about much more than coffee.

First woman: It looks lovely, looks, ah, especially for the boxes, to keep the boxes, the old phone boxes. It's a very good idea.

Café employee: It (³   ) a sense of community. I think without this here, from what I've noticed, there is no one place where people can come together and meet and just chit-chat.

Second woman: I think it's absolutely brilliant. Um, we did, we just (⁴   ) (⁵   ) for a coffee and we didn't realise it was a telephone box.

North: But the coffee box has problems. So, (⁶   ) a coffee, the owner explained all.

Mustafa Mehmet, Café owner: We can sell coffee, we can sell snacks, um, cold drinks, books, flowers if we wanted to.

North: But there are rules.

Mehmet: For us to be able to sell coffee here is, we have to go inside the box. We have to have a (⁷   ) to come in the box, make the coffee, take the money or, and have the door closed. That's the only way we're allowed to sell.

5

10

15

20

25

30

North: So there's no problem with you selling the coffee.

Mehmet: No problem whatsoever selling the coffee, as long as we're inside the phone box.

North: How do you feel about that? 35

Mehmet: I feel that's ridiculous (*laughs*).

North: Because once you've got the cups, the machine, and the milk in the phone box, anything else is a bit of a (^{8}).

Mehmet: A guy from the council come down. He turned up and said to me, "Well, what you're doing is (^{9}) (^{10}) (^{11}). 40 You can't be selling coffee standing here. "Um, he (^{12}) me with a fixed (^{13}) fine for £150. So I ignored him. Then two days after, he came back again and (^{14}) another fine for £150. And I, again I like said, "Well I'm not p-, I'm not paying these." So I ignored him again. Then he turned up a third time and (^{15}) us with another fine, 45 of £150. So that's four now, eh, three.

North: That's a lot of coffee you've got to sell.

Mehmet: That's a lot of coffee I have to sell.

North: Some might say that the idea is lovely, but you're getting cheap rent for a (^{16}) position, and you're breaking the rules. 50

Mehmet: Before we started selling coffee here, the council knew exactly what we were going to do. So if it was a big (^{17}) at the time, why didn't they bring it up?

North: Hounslow Council told us anyone trading on the street must have a street trading licence, and we found that Mr. Mehmet was trading without one. He's 55 since (^{18}) an application for a licence and this is being (^{19}) by the council.

North: Mustapha finds out next week whether his café can stay. He says any risk's worth taking for (^{20}) (^{21}) the box. Emma North, BBC London News.   (*Tuesday 4 September 2018*) 60

Notes ···
l. 5: **Harrods** 「ハロッズ」ロンドンのブロンプトンにあるヨーロッパ有数のデパート。1840年代に創業 l. 6: **Harvey Nichols** 「ハーヴェイ・ニコルズ」ロンドンのナイツブリッジのスローン街にある、婦人子供服で知られる高級デパート。1831年創業 l. 12: **Turnham Green** 「ターナム・グリーン」ロンドン西部ハウンズロウ地区チズィックにある地下鉄の駅名 l. 54: **Hounslow** 「ハウンズロウ」大ロンドン西部のテムズ川沿いの区

青い電話ボックス

　赤い電話ボックスが有名なイギリスですが、実は、青い電話ボックスも存在します。police boxと呼ばれ、警察関係者や市民の緊急連絡用に、地元の警察署直通の電話が備え付けられています。イギリスで最初のポリス・ボックスは、19世紀末、スコットランド南西部の街グラスゴーに設置されました。初期型のボックスは六角形で縦長の狭い設備で、色も赤く塗られていましたが、20世紀になると、より大型の四角く青いボックスが設置されるようになりました。赤い電話ボックス同様、青いボックスも今では使われなくなってしまいました。しかし、BBCの有名SFドラマシリーズ『ドクター・フー』（*Doctor Who*, 1963- ）に登場するタイムマシン「ターディス（TARDIS）」の外観がポリス・ボックスを模したものであることなどから、なおも根強い人気があります。

▶▶▶ Moving On

6 Making a Summary

CD1-04

Fill the gaps to complete the summary.

　　People have found many (c　　　　　) ways to give London's red phone boxes a new (l　　　　) of life. One in Turnham Green is causing a bit of a (s　　　　　). It has been converted into a café, selling coffee. People like it because it looks lovely, and it adds a sense of (c　　　　　). However, it is against the law, because the employee and customer should be inside the box with the door closed. Of course, that would be a bit of a (s　　　　　), but the council has (i　　　　　) the café owner with three fixed (p　　　　) fines of £150 each. He said he was not going to pay them, but he has (s　　　　) an application for a street trading licence. He doesn't feel guilty about having such a (p　　　　) trading spot, because the council knew that he was going to sell coffee, but they didn't think it was a big (i　　　　　). In any case, the owner believes the risk was worth taking for thinking outside the box.

7 Follow Up

Discuss, write or present.

1. What do you think about the phone box café? Would you like to have a cup of coffee there?

2. Can you think of any other interesting ways to use old phone boxes? Try to be imaginative.

3. The council has fined the café owner because the rules say customers should be inside, but he has refused to pay, and so he has a prime position with cheap rent. Which side are you on? Discuss the situation with your partner.

Unit 2
Breakdancing at the Olympics

2020年東京大会後のオリンピック新種目として、ブレイクダンスが検討されています。新競技の現場で期待に胸を膨らませる人たちのインタビューを見てみましょう。

▶ Starting Off

1 Setting the Scene

▌ What do you think?

1. How do you feel about dancing? Do you like to dance, or watch dancing? What kind of dancing do you like?
2. What do you know about breakdancing? Is it something that you would like to try?
3. Where and when are the next Olympics going to be held? What about the Olympics after that? What Olympic events are there, and which ones do you like the best?

2 Building Language

▌ Which word (1-6) best fits which explanation (a-f)?

1. dizzying   [   ]   a. play or dance to music in an informal way
2. jam   [   ]   b. so extreme that you feel unsteady
3. agility   [   ]   c. a distinctive character or attitude
4. dedication   [   ]   d. a plan of dance moves and steps
5. choreography   [   ]   e. the power to move quickly and easily
6. ethos   [   ]   f. commitment and devotion to something

▶▶ Watching the News

3 Understanding Check 1

▌ Read the quotes, then watch the news and match them to the right people.

1. . . . well that remains to be seen. [   ]

2. Whoa! You know, I want to, I want to do this.   [   ]

3. I want to be like them, but in breaking kind of style.   [   ]

4. So for me, it makes sense.   [   ]

4 Understanding Check 2

▌ Which is the best answer?

1. Which of the following is <u>not</u> true about breakdancing?
   a. Breakdancing is now focused on competition.
   b. Breakdancers must be strong, agile and dedicated.
   c. Breakdancing is an event at the Tokyo Olympics.
   d. Breakdancers are becoming ambitious.

2. What will take place in 2024?
   a. the Paris Olympics
   b. the World Breakdancing Games
   c. the New York Olympics
   d. the Paris Breakdance Competition

3. What is the ethos of the Olympics?
   a. stronger, smoother, longer
   b. faster, smoother, longer
   c. faster, higher, longer
   d. faster, higher, stronger

4. According to the reporter, what does breakdancing require?

_____

5. Why does it make sense to the man in a blue T-shirt and cream hat that breakdancing should be an Olympic event?

_____

6. What does the young girl want to feel like?

_____

●●Background Information●●

　今回のニュースは、2024年7月26日から8月11日にかけて開催されるパリ・オリンピックの競技種目に「ブレイクダンス (breaking)」が選ばれる可能性が濃厚だという話題でした。スケートボード、スポーツクライミング、サーフィンと共にブレイクダンスが選出される理由は、この種目がオリンピック競技をよりジェンダーのバランスの良いものにし、より若々しくより都会的にするという、2020年のオリンピック・アジェンダに則っているからです。一方、スカッシュ、ビリヤード、チェスは競技種目に選ばれず、2020年東京大会で初めて選ばれた空手も落選の模様です。

　ブレイクダンスは、2018年にアルゼンチンのブエノスアイレスで行われた「ユースオリンピック (the Youth Olympic Games)」で初めて競技種目に選ばれ、男子はロシアのセルゲイ・チェルニシェフ (Sergei Chernyshev) 選手、女子は日本の河合来夢選手が優勝しました。イギリスはこの大会には代表選手を送りませんでしたが、10歳からブレイクダンスを始め、世界大会で活躍するカラム・シン (Karam Singh) 選手のような有力選手もいます。競技は1対1の対戦形式で行われ、身体的能力、音楽性、個性や創造性などが採点基準に挙げられていますが、採点の不透明さが懸念されています。

　競技種目の最終決定は2020年12月の国際オリンピック委員会執行役員会によりますが、ニュースにあるように、現場はすでに盛り上がりを見せているのです。

参考：https://www.bbc.com/sport/olympics/47317052
　　　https://www.bbc.com/sport/olympics/47317059
　　　https://www.olympics.org/news/ioc-executive-board-accepts-paris-2024-proposal-for-new-sports

5 Filling Gaps — News Story

⊙ CD1-05 [Original] ⊙ CD1-06 [Voiced]

Watch the news, then fill the gaps in the text.

Richard Conway: It's enough to make your head (^{1}). Breakdancing, or breaking as it's more commonly known has (^{2}) from the basements and streets of New York in the 1970s, and is now headed to the (^{3}) heights of the Paris Games in 2024.

Stan Blake, breaker: Breaking's come from such a small thing, and in such a (^{4}) (^{5}) of time. Like it came from all, just people in the Bronx, just (^{6}) and stuff and it's come up to this (^{7}) thing, people are going to see it in the Olympics and be (^{8}) like "Whoa! You know, I want to, I want to do this".

Conway: But while it requires strength, (^{9}) and (^{10}), is it really (^{11}) of a place at an Olympics?

Jonzi D, Artistic Director, Breakin' Convention: This dance is so (^{12}) on competition. For the last 20, 25 years we've seen people (^{13}) and dancing as though their moves are weapons. So for me, it makes sense. What I mean is there's no reason why it shouldn't go up to that level.

Conway: Breaking is going from the streets to the (^{14}) where it will get its chance to shine in Paris in 2024. Whether it can (^{15}) on the podium at the Olympics, well that remains to be seen.

Conway: Now the decision to include breaking in Paris has given B-boys and B-girls across the country golden ambitions for the future.

B-Girl Terra, breaker: When I saw, like, Usain Bolt or Mo Farah. And they like,

10

15

20

25

30

5

they're running in the (^{16})
and they get that (^{17}), and
they stand up on like, those things.
That's what I want to feel like. I want to
be like them, but in breaking kind of
style.

35

Conway: The Olympics is welcoming a new (^{18}) to its age-old
(^{19}) of faster, higher, stronger. As the world turns, so too must   40
the (^{20}). Richard Conway, BBC news.

(*Wednesday 20 February 2019*)

Notes..

l. 11: **the Bronx** 「ブロンクス」ニューヨーク市北部の自治区。マンハッタン島の北東、本土にある   l. 17:
Jonzi D 「ジョンズィD」劇作家・ダンサー。ブレイキング・コンヴェンションの創設当初からの芸術監督   l.
17: **Breakin' Convention** 「ブレイキング・コンヴェンション」2004年よりロンドンのサドラーズウェル
ズ劇場（Sadler's Wells Theatre）のプロデュースで毎年開催されているブレイクダンスの競技会   l. 26: **the**
podium 「舞台」古代神殿や円形闘技場が建つ高い土台。オリンピック発祥の古代ギリシャを想起させる   l.
28: **B-boys and B-girls** 「BボーイズやBガールズ」ヒップホップやラップ・ミュージックのダンサーや演奏
家、およびファンの若者を指す   l. 31: **B-Girl Terra** 「Bガールテラ」2007年イギリス生まれのダンサー。
幼少期にヒップホップを始め、数々の賞を受賞している   l. 32: **Usain Bolt** 「ウサイン・ボルト（1986- ）」
ジャマイカの元陸上競技短距離選手。2012年のロンドン・オリンピックを含む2002年から2017年までの現役
時代に数々の記録を樹立し、「人類史上最高のスプリンター（the greatest sprinter of all time）」と評された
l. 32: **Mo Farah** 「モウ・ファラー（1983- ）」本名モハメド（Mohammed）・ファラー。ソマリア出身のイ
ギリスの陸上競技中長距離選手。ロンドン・オリンピックでの5,000メートルと10,000メートルの金メダルを
含む数々のレースを制覇し、2017年に爵位を受けた

Behind the Scenes

「スポーツ」の語源

　日本語で「スポーツ」といえば、体を使った運動や競技が思い浮かびます。しかし、英語のsportは古フランス語で「気晴らし」「楽しみ」を意味するdesportに由来しており、本来、面白いものや娯楽となるもの全般を指す言葉です。そのため、ラグビーやサッカー、マラソンといった競技だけでなく、今回のニュースで取り上げられたブレイクダンス、狩猟、乗馬、ダーツ、ビリヤード、チェスやその他のボードゲームといった、多種多様な競技やゲームをsportとして見なすことが可能です。ちなみに、近年知名度が増している「eスポーツ（eSports）」は「エレクトロニック・スポーツ（electronic sports）」の略称で、コンピュータ・ゲームを用いた競技のことを指します。

▶▶▶ Moving On

6 Making a Summary

❙ Fill the gaps to complete the summary.

　　Breakdancing, now better known as breaking, began in the streets of the Bronx, New York, where people started (j　　　　　) to music. It requires (a　　　　　), strength, and (d　　　　　). Now, it has been chosen as an event at the (d　　　　　) heights of the Paris 2024 Olympic Games, where the (e　　　　) is 'faster, higher, stronger'. For Jonzi D, the Artistic Director of Breakin' Convention, being in the Olympics makes sense, as breaking is (f　　　　　) on competition, and dancers (c　　　　　　) their moves as if they are weapons. B-Girl Terra, a young breaker, wants to feel like Usain Bolt or Mo Farah, collecting their medals after running in the wind.

7 Follow Up

❙ Discuss, write or present.

1. Do you agree that breakdancing should be an Olympic event? Find out what other people in your class think. Will you watch it?

2. When the Olympics are held in Tokyo in 2020, baseball, softball, surfing, skateboarding, karate and sports climbing will be included in the events. Do you think these sports suit the Olympic ethos? Are there any other sports that you think should be included?

3. B-Girl Terra says she wants to feel like Usain Bolt or Mo Farah. They are her sporting heroes. Do you have any sporting heroes that you would like to copy? How would it feel to be like them?

Shopping without Plastic

スーパーマーケットの商品に付き物のプラスチック容器ですが、環境問題の一因となっています。廃止の取り組みはどのようなものなのでしょうか。あるスーパーの例を見てみましょう。

▶ Starting Off

1 Setting the Scene

▌ **What do you think?**

1. Are you worried about the amount of plastic pollution that we produce? What harm does it do? Do you think that we should do something about it?

2. When you go shopping, how much plastic is used in the items you buy? Why do you think that there is so much plastic in shops? What do they use it for?

3. How do you think that shops could reduce the amount of plastic that they use?

2 Building Language

▌ **Which word (1-5) best fits which explanation (a-e)?**

1. remerchandise [   ]   **a.** ready; no need for any preparation
2. good-to-go   [   ]   **b.** a company or person that provides and delivers
3. scheme   [   ]   something
4. absorb   [   ]   **c.** plan for and promote the sale of something again
5. supplier   [   ]   **d.** accept something without being harmed
                            e. a plan of action to be followed

3 Understanding Check 1

| Read the quotes, then watch the news and match them to the right people.

1. It's not a big cost.   [   ]

2. . . . it is going to be difficult for us to change.   [   ]

3. . . . some shoppers can leave with a completely plastic-free basket of shopping.   [   ]

4. Some of the packages in this store don't look plastic-free but they are.

                                     [   ]

4 Understanding Check 2

| Which is the best answer?

1. What supermarket do we see in the news story?
   a. Thornton's Budgens in Belsize Park, South East London
   b. Thornton's Belsize in Budgen's Park, North West London
   c. Thornton's Belsize in Budgen's Park, South East London
   d. Thornton's Budgens in Belsize Park, North West London

2. Why is this supermarket special?
   a. It is recycling all of its plastic packaging.
   b. It has replaced much of its plastic packaging with natural materials.
   c. It is giving away free plastic packaging.
   d. It has organised all its plastic products so it is easier to shop.

3. How much is this costing the supermarket?
   a. It costs a little bit more.
   b. It costs a lot more.
   c. It costs about the same as before.
   d. It actually costs slightly less than before.

4. How can you dispose of cellulose packaging?

_____

5. According to the woman in the environmental group, why is it going to be difficult for us to change?

_____

6. How does the supermarket owner think that costs will go down?

_____

●●Background Information●●

　今回のニュースは、イギリスのスーパーマーケットに「プラスチックを使わない（plastic-free)」容器に入った商品の売り場が設けられたという話題でした。その背景には、プラスチックごみをめぐる問題が存在しています。カリフォルニア大学のローランド・ガイヤー博士らが発表した論文によると、これまでに世界で83億トンのプラスチックが生成され、2015年の時点で63億トンのプラスチックごみが生み出されました。これらのプラスチックごみのうち、9%がリサイクル、12%が焼却、79%が埋め立て地や自然環境中に堆積されています。そして、プラスチック製造と廃棄が現状のまま続くと、2050年までには120億トンのプラスチックごみが埋め立て地や自然環境中に存在することになります。

　2010年に国立生態学分析統合センターとジョージア大学の科学者らが行った研究によると、毎年、1,000万トンのプラスチックが海に流入しており、海鳥、海亀、イルカ、アザラシのような大きな海洋生物にとっての脅威となっています。例えば、海亀はプラスチックの袋と餌のクラゲを見分けることができず、間違って食べてしまった結果、体内にプラスチックが詰まって死んでしまうことがあります。また、プラスチックごみは時が経つと次第に生物分解し、「マイクロプラスチック（micro-plastic)」という微細なプラスチック片になりますが、それを魚が食べ、さらに人間がその魚を食べることによる影響が懸念されています。

　こうした現状を踏まえて、イギリス政府は2018年1月、2042年までに全ての回避可能なプラスチックごみを根絶すると発表しました。その方法としては、①今回のニュースのように、各スーパーマーケットにプラスチック・フリーの売り場を導入する、②プラスチックの使い捨て持ち帰り容器に課税する、③現行のプラスチック製レジ袋に対する5ペンスの課税を延長する、④「プラスチック改革（plastics innovation)」のための政府の基金を創設する、などがありますが、これらの提案に法的効力がないことや、25年という達成目標期間が長すぎることを指摘する反対意見があります。世界中の人々にとって、プラスチックごみ問題は待ったなしの課題なのです。

参考：https://www.bbc.com/news/science-environment-42264788
　　　https://www.bbc.com/news/science-environment-42639359

5 Filling Gaps   News Story

▌ Watch the news, then fill the gaps in the text.

Newsreader: A supermarket in North West London has become one of the first in the world to offer entirely plastic-free (¹   ). Thornton's Budgens in Belsize Park now says some shoppers can leave with a completely plastic-free basket of shopping. It says it wants bigger companies to follow its (²   ). Victoria Cook has been to look inside.

5

Victoria Cook: This looks like a normal supermarket in Belsize Park. But come inside, and you can start to notice a difference. The owner says this is one of the world's first (³   ) where you can do your weekly shopping plastic-free. Much of the packaging has been replaced with natural (⁴   ). This is sugarcane and cornstarch.

10

Cook: Some of the packages in this store don't look plastic-free but they are. So, these, for example, and this one, when you look inside, it's actually made of cellulose and paper. So, all of these can go into your garden compost, and they'll (⁵   ) (⁶   ) in around 15 weeks. The owner says it's been (⁷   ), but necessary.

15

Andrew Thornton, owner of Thornton's Budgens: The whole store had to be (⁸   ), to organise the products, to sort the plastic from the non-plastic. So, it can be done. And, you know, if we can do it, with our one shop and our (⁹   ) (¹⁰   ), what do you think, one of the big guys, a Tesco or Sainsbury's, if they said, "We're going to do this"? They could do it too.

20

25

Cook: The store worked (¹¹   ) an environmental group to make the changes.

Frankie Gillard, A Plastic Planet: This feels and sounds like plastic, but it's actually cellulose.

30

Sian Sutherland, A Plastic Planet: Here we have a (¹²   ) of how change

can happen, and it is, it is going to be difficult for us to change. We're so, you know, we're so used to being able to buy things in their easy, you, (^{13}) way. And that's, that is what this is all about, it's being a (^{14}) for that change.

Cook: Although the (^{15}) gone down well with customers, it is costing the business slightly more.

Thornton: It's not a big cost. We're (^{16}) that at the moment and we hope that, you know, with (^{17}) (^{18}) and, and also with more people doing it, that the cost will come down.

Cook: Now the (^{19}) here want to go further. They're trying to convince more of their (^{20}) to go plastic-free. Victoria Cook, BBC London News.

(*Monday 19 November 2018*)

Notes ··

l. 4: **Thornton's Budgens**「ソーントンズ・バジェンズ」独自ブランドの商品や国産オーガニック食品などを売るバジェンズ・スーパーマーケットチェーンの1店舗　l. 5: **Belsize Park**「ベルサイズ・パーク」ロンドン北西部カムデン地区にある地域　l. 17: **cellulose**「セルロース」樹木などの繊維素　l. 17: **compost**「コンポスト」堆肥、培養土。ここでは庭に置いて生ゴミや野菜屑などを入れ、堆肥を作るための容器compost bin を指す　l. 24: **Tesco**「テスコ」イギリスの大手スーパーマーケットチェーン。1919年創業　l. 24: **Sainsbury's**「セインズベリー」イギリスの大手スーパーマーケットチェーン。1869年創業　l. 28: **A Plastic Planet**「プラスチック・プラネット」プラスチック容器の廃止を促進する環境慈善団体

使い捨てレジ袋の歴史

　プラスチック製レジ袋の原料であるポリエチレンは、1933年、イングランド北西部のノースウィッチ（Northwich）にある化学工場で偶然発見されて以来、工業用に広く用いられるようになりました。1960年代、スウェーデンの技術者ステン・グスタフ・チューリン（Sten Gustaf Thulin）が、後に「Tシャツ型プラスチックバッグ（T-shirt plastic bag）」と呼ばれることとなる、取っ手のついたポリエチレン製レジ袋を開発しました。便利で軽量なレジ袋は瞬く間にヨーロッパや世界中に普及し、イングランドでも長年多くの買い物客に無料で配布されてきました。しかし、2015年、スーパーマーケットや小売店等でのレジ袋の有料化が義務づけられると、その消費量は以後3年間で約80％も減少しました。エコバッグを持参する人が大半となった今、レジ袋の時代は終わりを迎えつつあります。

▶▶▶ Moving On

6 Making a Summary

CD1-10

▮ Fill the gaps to complete the summary.

　A London supermarket is offering (e　　　　) plastic-free zones, so shoppers can leave with a plastic-free basket of shopping. It looks normal, but packaging has been replaced with natural materials, like sugarcane, cornstarch, paper and (c　　　　), which can go into your garden (c　　　　). The store had to be (r　　　　　　), to sort plastic from non-plastic, but it is able to (a　　　　) the small extra cost, which might go down when sales increase. It is going to be difficult to change, because we are so used to being able to buy (g　　　　　　) products, but the (s　　　　) has gone down well with customers, and the staff hope their (s　　　　) will follow its (l　　　).

7 Follow Up

▮ Discuss, write or present.

1. How do you feel about this store? Do you think you would shop there? Why or why not? How successful would it be in Japan?

2. Do you think that more stores all over the world will follow the lead of this store, and use less plastic in order to protect the environment?

3. What else can be done to reduce plastic waste in Japan? What about other types of waste that are harming the environment?

Unit 4
Edinburgh to Tax Tourists

グローバル化の進む世界で、情報・物品の流通や人の交流も盛んになっています。観光業が大規模になる中で、観光税導入の動きがあります。ニュースを見てみましょう。

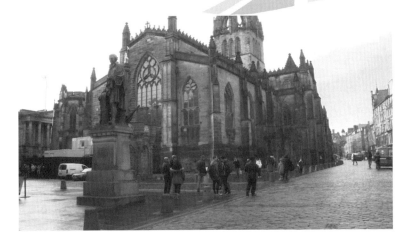

▶ Starting Off

1 Setting the Scene

▌ **What do you think?**

1. Talk or write about some places you have been to. Why did you go there?
2. Do you find being a tourist expensive? What sort of things do you have to pay for?
3. What sort of problems might tourists cause in the places that they visit? Can you think of some examples?

2 Building Language

▌ **For each word (1-6), find two synonyms (a-l).**

1. appeal	[/]		**a.** work	**g.** tenable
2. function	[/]		**b.** unequal	**h.** explain
3. impact	[/]		**c.** burden	**i.** worthwhile
4. disproportionate	[/]		**d.** unfair	**j.** charm
5. clarify	[/]		**e.** operate	**k.** simplify
6. sustainable	[/]		**f.** attractiveness	**l.** effect

3 Understanding Check 1

❙ Read the quotes, then watch the news and match them to the right people.

1. ... through that relatively organised chaos that the festival becomes. [   ]

2. For, you know, hotels, this is nothing. For us, it's a big deal. [   ]

3. ... obviously Scotland or the UK is a beautiful country ... [   ]

4. Now, councillors in Edinburgh have voted in favour ... [   ]

4 Understanding Check 2

❙ Which is the best answer?

1. What is the plan for the Edinburgh tourist tax?
   a. to charge every tourist an extra £2 per night
   b. to add £2 to the bill for every room per night
   c. to add 2% to the bill in hotels, B&Bs and hostels
   d. to charge hotels, B&Bs and hostels £2 per night

2. Which of the following was <u>not</u> mentioned as a reason for the tourist tax?
   a. The city can control the number of tourists.
   b. It could help the council cope with the costs of mass tourism.
   c. Tourists should pay for all the culture that Edinburgh offers.
   d. The council will be able to keep the streets clean.

3. Why can't the tourist tax start immediately?
   a. Many other cities have to watch its progress.
   b. We need a new attempt to make mass tourism sustainable.
   c. The right legislation has not yet been enabled.
   d. There is a concern about young travellers on tight budgets.

▎What do you remember?

4. What did the first woman think about the tourist tax?

---

5. How did the Leader of Edinburgh City Council describe the Edinburgh Festival?

---

6. The hostel owner was worried about the effect of the tax. He said it would be disproportionate. What did he mean?

●●Background Information●●

　今回のニュースは、世界有数の観光都市であるスコットランドのエディンバラが、イギリス初となる「観光税（tourist tax）」の導入を検討しているという話題でした。同様の観光税は、キプロス、デンマーク、エストニア、フィンランド、アイルランド、ラトヴィア、ルクセンブルク、スウェーデンなど、イギリスを除くEU加盟国の3分の2の国々で導入されており、国全体、もしくは特定の都市や地域に課されています。

　エディンバラを訪れる観光客は過去5年間で18%増加して385万人となり、ごみや混雑の問題が生じています。このような状況においてエディンバラは1,160万ポンド（16億2,400万円、1ポンド＝140円）から1,460万ポンド（20億4,400万円）の税収を見込み、観光税の導入を提案しました。

　エディンバラ市議会が、合わせて2,500を超える住民と企業に観光税導入の賛否を問うアンケート調査を行ったところ、90%の住民は賛成、51%の宿泊所提供者も賛成で、全体の9%のみが反対、という結果でした。2019年2月、エディンバラ市議会は43対15の賛成多数で観光税の導入を可決しましたが、20%という高い付加価値税（VAT＝value-added tax）をすでに課しているスコットランド政府は、観光税がスコットランドの競争力を弱め、経済成長を損なうとの理由で反対しており、この法案が議会を通過するかどうかは不明です。

参考：https://www.bbc.com/news/uk-scotland-45511022

https://www.bbc.com/news/uk-scotland-edinburgh-east-fife-46797446

https://www.bbc.com/news/uk-scotland-47157011

http://www.gbrmpa.gov.au/

▌ **Watch the news, then fill the gaps in the text.**

Newsreader: Now, councillors in Edinburgh have voted in favour of introducing a tourist tax, which will be the first of its kind in the UK. The plan is to (^{1}) an extra £2 per room, per night, in hotels, B&Bs and hostels. Our Scotland correspondent, James Shaw, has more.

5

James Shaw: Arriving in Edinburgh, the Scottish capital and one of the hottest tourist (^{2}) in the UK. It seems to get more popular every year. But what difference would a tourist tax make to the city's (^{3})? 10

First woman: I don't see how it's going to (^{4}) like more tourists coming into the country, because, obviously Scotland or the UK is a beautiful country but, if there's more tax and if the (^{5}) going to be more expensive then, it's, I think it would definitely discourage, um, more people. 15

Shaw: There are strong arguments (^{6}) (^{7}) (^{8}). Visitors and residents acknowledge that something needs to be done, but is this the right way to do it?

Second woman: Well, I would hope that the council would think about spending it on, um, keeping the streets clean. 20

First man: That's terrible, ha, ha, a tourist tax!

Second man: There's a lot of culture, they offer a lot for the people. So, it's good to pay for it.

Shaw: Do you think it would discourage people (^{9}) (^{10}) to your city? 25

Third man: Yeah, I think it would, definitely.

Shaw: But council leaders believe there may be no other way to (^{11}) (^{12}) the costs which mass tourism brings to the city.

30

Adam McVey, Leader of Edinburgh City Council: It's about how we make sure the city continues to (^{13}), through that relatively organised chaos that the festival becomes.

35

Shaw: There is a concern about the (^{14}) for young travellers on tight (^{15}).

Hostel owner: We just really want to make our voice heard as a hostel specifically. The £2 tax per person, per booking, er, will (^{16}) affect hostel guests and people who tend to travel on a (^{17}). For, you know, 40 hotels, this is nothing. For us, it's a big deal. It's £2 on top of a booking that's £10, and that's 20%. So, you know, that needs to be (^{18}) for us.

Shaw: The tourism tax will not (^{19}) (^{20}) (^{21}) for a while. The Scottish parliament still needs to pass enabling legislation. But, many cities in the UK will be watching the progress of this new attempt 45 to make mass tourism (^{22}). James Shaw, BBC News, Edinburgh.

(Thursday 7 February 2019)

Notes ··

l. 1: **Edinburgh**「エディンバラ」スコットランドの首都　l. 6: **B&Bs** 朝食付き民宿でbed and breakfast の略　l. 6: **hostels**「ホステル」主に青年旅行者用の簡易宿泊所　l. 35: **the festival** 最も有名なものは8月 に開催されるエディンバラ国際フェスティバル〈次ページ参照〉だが、年間を通じて様々なフェスティバルが開 催されている

フェスティバルの街、エディンバラ

　エディンバラでは年間を通じて様々なフェスティバルが開催されています。中でも「エディンバラ国際フェスティバル（Edinburgh International Festival）」は世界最大規模の芸術の祭典です。毎年夏に3週間にわたって開催され、演劇、オペラ、ダンス、クラシック音楽といった伝統的な分野で活躍する芸術家たちが世界中から招かれて公演を行います。また、毎年同時期に開催される「エディンバラ・フェスティバル・フリンジ（Edinburgh Festival Fringe）」も同じく芸術の祭典ですが、こちらは資格を問わず誰でも演者として参加できるのが特徴で、コメディや大道芸など、幅広い分野のパフォーマーたちが街中いたるところで腕前を披露しています。

▶▶▶ Moving On

6 Making a Summary

Fill the gaps to complete the summary.

Edinburgh is considering the introduction of a tourist tax, of £2 per room per night. The city hope that this will help with the costs of tourism, and make sure it can (f　　　) during the festival. One resident hopes the money will be used to keep the streets clean. However, some people worry whether the tax might reduce Edinburgh's (a　　　). One tourist said that if accommodation becomes more expensive, it would discourage tourists. In particular, there might be an (i　　　) on travellers on (t　　　) budgets. A hostel owner felt his guests might be (d　　　　　) affected, because they would pay the same tax as guests in expensive hotels. The tax won't be in force until (l　　　　) has been passed, but other cities are also interested in how it might make mass tourism (s　　　　　).

7 Follow Up

Discuss, write or present.

1. Do you think it is fair to charge tourists an extra tax? Would it discourage you from going and staying somewhere?
2. At the beginning of this unit you thought of some problems that tourists cause. Do you think that a tax like this could solve these problems?
3. Do you know if Japanese cities with lots of tourists, such as Kyoto, have introduced similar taxes? Please research how they spend the income from these taxes.

Unit **5**
A Four-Day Week

テクノロジーの進歩により週4日勤務が実現しそうですが、人々の生活はどのように変化するのでしょうか。ニュースを見てみましょう。

▶ Starting Off

1 Setting the Scene

▌ **What do you think?**

1. How many days a week do you study, or work? Is the number the same as most people?
2. Would you prefer to work or study for fewer days in a week? Why or why not?
3. Can you think of any reasons why employers might prefer their employees to work only four days a week?

2 Building Language

▌ **For each word (1-6), find two synonyms (a-l).**

1. boost [/]		**a.** useful	**g.** principles
2. productive [/]		**b.** order	**h.** command
3. conscience [/]		**c.** risk	**i.** duty
4. dispute [/]		**d.** argument	**j.** encouragement
5. dictate [/]		**e.** quarrel	**k.** creative
6. threat [/]		**f.** danger	**l.** support

3 Understanding Check 1

❚ Read the quotes, then watch the news and match them to the right people.

1. ... unions want them to share the benefits by giving the staff more time off. [   ]

2. It's got to start somewhere, all these things have to start somewhere ... [   ]

3. We felt that we were, had an opportunity to prove something that I felt was true ... [   ]

4. ... which I just probably wouldn't have the time or the energy to do, otherwise. [   ]

4 Understanding Check 2

❚ Which is the best answer?

1. What does the TUC want?
   a. It wants the government to solve the problems of new technology.
   b. It wants workers to have a shorter working week for the same pay.
   c. It wants to force businesses to pay their workforce more.
   d. It wants the government to train more people to use artificial intelligence.

2. What happened when Royal Mail introduced more sorting machines?
   a. Bosses and shareholders kept the extra cash.
   b. The postal workers' working week increased to 39 hours.
   c. The unions shared the benefits.
   d. The postal workers' union fought for staff to get more time off.

3. Which of the following sentences expresses the conclusion correctly?
   a. Whether technological change will have good or bad effects depends on the attitudes of companies.
   b. Companies' attitudes in the future will depend on the role of technology.
   c. In the years ahead, every industry will give a treat to the workforce.
   d. Companies are dictating attitudes concerning the bigger role of industry.

▎What do you remember?

4. Why does the owner of the photo studio think that a four-day week is a good idea?

_____

5. What happened in the Swedish trial of six-hour working days?

_____

6. According to the man from the postal workers' union, why should the union not ignore this issue?

_____

●●Background Information●●

　イギリスでは週5日、1日8時間労働が基本ですが、労働組合会議（the TUC: Trades Union Congress）が2018年に発表した調査結果によると、実に140万人以上が週7日にわたって働いており、週45時間以上働いている人の数は330万人にのぼることがわかりました。また、労働者の多くが、賃金や長時間労働、仕事上のストレスによって悩みを抱えていることも明らかとなり、働き方の見直しが求められつつあります。

　労働日数や労働時間の削減は、働く人々にどのような利益をもたらすでしょうか。今回のニュースでは、スウェーデンのヨーテボリの実例について触れていました。ヨーテボリでは、2015年から2017年までの2年間、市内のある介護施設において、これまでの1日8時間から6時間への労働時間短縮の試験運用が行われました。すると、職員の健康状態が改善し、病気による欠勤が減少するとともに、作業効率や労働意欲の向上が見られたということです。しかし、その反面、17名の従業員を追加で雇わねばならず、約1,200万クローナ（約107万ポンド）という多大な費用がかかりました。結果として、永続的な6時間労働の実現は困難と判断され、本格的な導入は中止となりました。

　このように、労働時間削減の長期的な運用には課題があります。しかし、AIや自動化、ロボットなどの新たなテクノロジーを導入することで、作業効率の向上と労働者の負担の軽減、生産性の拡大などが実現し、イギリスの国内総生産（GDP）は今後10年間で少なくとも2,000億ポンド（約28兆円）引き上げられることが見込まれています。労働者の81%が労働時間の短縮を望む中、45%は、これまでの賃金を維持したまま勤務日数を週4日に減らすことを希望しており、テクノロジーがその支えとなることに大きな期待を寄せています。

　もっとも、新しいテクノロジーの到来に不安を感じる労働者も少なくありません。AIやロボットが人間に取って代わることによって失業者が増加するのではないかという懸念や、拡大した利益を経営者層が独占することを危惧する声もあり、テクノロジーがもたらす恩恵を広く公平に分配する必要性が叫ばれています。

参考：https://www.tuc.org.uk/news/tuc-calls-new-tech-pave-way-shorter-working-week-and-higher-pay
　　　https://www.independent.co.uk/news/business/news/sweden-six-hour-working-day-too-expensive-scrapped-experiment-cothenburg-pilot-scheme-a7508581.html

❚ Watch the news, then fill the gaps in the text.

Newsreader: Technology means that a four-day working week will be possible in the future, so long as businesses are forced to (^{1}) the benefits of new technology with their (^{2}). That's the (^{3}) from the TUC, which is using its annual (^{4}) to call on the government to take action to help people work less but still get paid the same. They (^{5}) artificial intelligence, robotics and automation could (^{6}) a major (^{7}) to the economy. Here's our business correspondent, Coletta Smith.

Photographer: Can you just hold it there for me?

Coletta Smith: The owners of this studio space in Cardiff are taking a different view of the working week. Staff get a full paycheck, but only work for four days.

Mark Hooper, owner of IndyCube: We felt that we were, had an opportunity to prove something that I felt was true, that people could be as (^{8}) in four days as five. If it does nothing more than has people who work for you who are less (^{9}), that will benefit us in (^{10}) at the ends of the day anyway because, you know, happier people work better.

Smith: Staff like Mari and Russ are making the most of their time off.

Mari Dunning, staff member of IndyCube: Sometimes if you use your day to get the hoovering done, and kind of get the house chores done, you've then got your weekend wide open and you, you're not kind of playing catch-up.

Russell Todd, staff member of IndyCube: It's rare I take a set day, if I'm honest. Um, it can be just working shorter days across the week.

Dunning: So, I write short stories and various different things which I just probably wouldn't have the time or the energy to do, otherwise.

5

15

10

20

25

30

Todd: It's terrific in managing your family commitments, you know, your school runs. You being there for those.

Dunning: Who doesn't want to work less hours if they can?

35

Smith: In Sweden, a trial of six-hour working days was stopped after the city of Gothenburg said it was too (^{11}) to buy in extra care workers. But could things be different in other industries?

40

Smith: When a company buys a new piece of technology and makes more money from it, rather than the bosses and the (^{12}) keeping that extra cash, unions want them to share the benefits by giving the staff more time off.

Smith: When new sorting machines were (^{13}) by Royal Mail, the postal workers' union fought for (^{14}) that to happen. 45
Their working week has now gone from 39 hours to 35 hours.

Terry Pullinger, Deputy General Secretary of the Communication Workers Union: If we ignored it, then that would be us, you know, ignoring our (^{15}) and just leaving it perhaps to another (^{16}), or somebody else. It's got to start somewhere, all these things have to start 50
somewhere, and that (^{17}) for us was a line in the sand.

Smith: It's clear that technology will play a bigger role in every industry in the years ahead. Companies' attitudes will (^{18}) if that will be a (^{19}), or a (^{20}) for the workforce. Coletta Smith, BBC News.

55

(Monday 10 September 2018)

Notes ···

l. 6: **the TUC (= Trades Union Congress)** 「労働組合会議」 48の労働組合が参加する、550万人の労働者を団結させるための組織。1868年創設　l. 13: **Cardiff** 「カーディフ」ウェールズの首都　l. 16: **IndyCube** 「インディキューブ」ウェールズで共同ワーキングスペースを運営する会社　l. 19: **at the ends of the day** 「結局、つまるところ」文法的に正しくはat the end of the day　l. 23: **the hoovering** 「掃除機をかけること」イギリス、フーバー（Hoover）社の電気掃除機から生じた単語　l. 38: **Gothenburg** 「ヨーテボリ」スウェーデンの港湾都市。人口約52万人　l. 44: **Royal Mail** 「ロイヤルメール」イギリスで郵便事業を営む公開有限会社　l. 47: **the Communication Workers Union** 「通信労働者組合」電信電話や郵便配達業界で働く人々のための労働組合。1995年設立

ユートピア、ディストピアと労働

　ユートピア文学の嚆矢であるトマス・モア（Thomas More, 1478-1535）の『ユートピア』（*Utopia*, 1516）では、世界中を航海した冒険家からの伝聞という形で理想社会の様子が語られます。ユートピアでは、人は1日6時間しか働かず、余暇は教養を高めることに当てることができる一方、奴隷制度など、後のディストピア文学へと発展する要素を含んでいます。ジョージ・オーウェル（George Orwell, 1903-50）がディストピア小説『1984年』（*1984*, 1948）で描く社会では、情報は絶えず改ざんされ、独裁者が意図的に作り出す永久戦争の状態の中、労働者階級がその短い生涯を通して身を粉にして働いても、物資は窮乏し、巷には犯罪が溢れています。

▶▶▶ Moving On

6 Making a Summary

▌ Fill the gaps to complete the summary.

　　The TUC claims that improvements in technology, such as (a ⎵⎵⎵⎵⎵⎵⎵) intelligence, robotics and automation, will provide a (b ⎵⎵⎵⎵⎵) to the economy. If companies share the benefits, it should mean that a four-day working week will soon be possible. As an example, after a (d ⎵⎵⎵⎵⎵⎵) when Royal Mail introduced new machines, the working week of postal workers decreased from 39 to 35 hours. The General Secretary of their union said that we should not ignore our (c ⎵⎵⎵⎵⎵), and this was a good place to start. Whether such technology change will be a (t ⎵⎵⎵⎵⎵) or a treat for workers will be (d ⎵⎵⎵⎵⎵) by the attitudes of companies. An owner of one such company said that a four-day week will not be a problem, as workers will be happier, and happier workers are more (p ⎵⎵⎵⎵⎵⎵). Two of his workers said that they were making the most of their time off.

7 Follow Up

▌ Discuss, write or present.

1. In what kind of industry do you think a four-day week could happen? Are there any industries where you think it couldn't happen? What technological changes might there be in the future? One day, do you think that nobody will need to work at all?

2. Do you agree that happier workers are more productive? If so, why do you think this is?

3. Two workers told us what they would do with their extra spare time. If you were given a four-day week, what would you do in your new spare time?

Unit **6**

The Fashion Industry and the Environment

安価でカジュアル、若者に人気のファストファッションですが、実は環境に悪影響を及ぼしています。企業にはどのような取り組みが求められているのでしょうか。ニュースを見てみましょう。

▶ Starting Off

1 Setting the Scene

▌ What do you think?

1. In what ways do humans harm the environment? Think of things you buy, and consider what product might have the worst effect.
2. With a partner, discuss the clothes that you are wearing now. When did you buy them? And how long do you think you will keep them?
3. What do you do with your clothes when you no longer want to wear them?

2 Building Language

▌ Which word (1-5) best fits which explanation (a-e)?

1. fuel   [   ]   **a.** throw away
2. junk   [   ]   **b.** stimulate; encourage; cause
3. incinerate [   ]   **c.** a very small piece of something
4. generate   [   ]   **d.** completely burn to ashes
5. fragment   [   ]   **e.** bring into existence; create or produce

3 Understanding Check 1

▌ Read the quotes, then watch the news and match them to the right people.

1. So that's give you an idea, the massive impact. [ ]

2. There's much more we can do and that's what we've said . . . [ ]

3. . . . when we have more clothes is that we're using them, we're wearing them less. [ ]

4. Every time I go to, out for shopping so I pick something up. [ ]

4 Understanding Check 2

▌ Which is the best answer?

1. Which of the following sentences is true?
   a. In the last 15 years, British purchases of clothes have doubled.
   b. British shoppers buy twice as many new clothes as any nation in Europe.
   c. In the last 15 years, fashion production has increased by £28 billion.
   d. Global production of clothing is double the British production of clothing.

2. What happens to most of the clothes and shoes that are thrown away?
   a. They are incinerated.
   b. They are resold.
   c. They are recycled.
   d. They are put into landfill.

3. There are lots of environmental and social problems with the fashion industry. Which of the following was <u>not</u> mentioned?
   a. Working conditions in the fashion industry are not good enough.
   b. Fragments of clothing are washed into the sea, where they are eaten.
   c. Many poor people in the world do not have enough clothing.
   d. Making clothes generates carbon emissions, which cause climate change.

What do you remember?

4. What has the government asked fashion retailers to do?

_____

5. Which three industries have a greater environmental impact than the clothing industry?

_____

6. What was the response of fashion retailers to the MPs' questions in the report?

_____

●●Background Information●●

　人気のファストファッションですが、数々の問題が指摘されています。イギリスの環境監査委員会 (the Environmental Audit Committee) は2018年秋、ファッション小売業界を代表する16の企業に対し、環境や社会への悪影響を軽減すべく、どのような行動や取り組みを行っているかの調査を行いました。調査内容は、有機栽培等、環境に優しいコットンを使った商品の製造や、危険な化学物質の排出制限、売れ残った商品の再利用またはリサイクルなど多岐に渡るものでした。そして、取り組みの度合いに応じ、各企業を①ほぼ取り組んでいない (least engaged)、②やや取り組んでいる (moderately engaged)、③概ね取り組んでいる (most engaged)、の3つに分類しました。

　結果、回答が不十分だったカート・ジェイガー (Kurt Geiger) を除く15社が評価を受けましたが、その内、アマゾンUK (Amazon UK)、JDスポーツ (JD Sports)、ブーフー (Boohoo) などの6社が、具体的な対策には「ほぼ取り組んでいない」とみなされました。これらの企業は、衣料品業界の環境への影響を軽減するための「持続可能な衣料品行動計画 (SCAP: Sustainable Clothing Action Plan)」に参加しておらず、二酸化炭素排出量や水の消費量、廃棄物の削減等への対策が不十分であると判断されました。また、同業界における労働者の生活賃金改善に向けての取り組みである「行動、協調、変化 (ACT: Action, Collaboration, Transformation)」にも関与しておらず、労働市場における対策の遅れが指摘される結果となりました。

　一方、「概ね取り組んでいる」とみなされたエイソス (ASOS)、マークス・アンド・スペンサー (Marks and Spencer)、テスコ (Tesco) などの5社に関しては、内4社がSCAPに参加しているほか、全社が環境に配慮した原料やリサイクル品を製造に使用し、不要となった製品の店頭回収に取り組んでいます。また、労働環境改善のための「倫理取引構想 (ETI: Ethical Trading Initiative)」に参加し、前向きな対策を行っている点も評価されました。しかし、総じて小売業界の対策の現状は不十分であると調査委員会は結論づけており、今後の改善が必要とされています。

参考：https://www.parliament.uk/business/committees/committees-a-z/commons-select/environmental-audit-committee/news-parliament-2017/sustainable-fashion-interim-report-published-17-19/

http://www.wrap.org.uk/sustainable-textiles/scap

▌ Watch the News, then fill the gaps in the text.

Newsreader: Some of Britain's leading fashion retailers are being asked by MPs to explain what they're doing to (^{1}) the environmental and social impact of their clothes and shoes. The Commons Environmental Audit Committee, says the clothing industry (^{2}) climate change, (^{3}) micro-plastics into the oceans and fills up landfill sites. Our environment analyst, Roger Harrabin reports.

5

10

Roger Harrabin: Fashion is (^{4}) £28 billion a year to the UK economy. MPs say British shoppers buy far more new clothes than any nation in Europe.

Mary Creagh MP, Labour: Clothing production has more than (^{5}) globally over the last 15 years. And in the UK, we're buying twice as much as we were buying 15 years ago. What that means when we have more clothes is that we're using them, we're wearing them less.

15

First woman: You have those go-to things, don't you? But, um, but I do get bored after, yeah, new, new fashions come in, new colours, new styles.

Second woman: Every time I go to, out for shopping so I pick something up.

20

Harrabin: But what happens to all these clothes that are loved and then (^{6})?

Harrabin: This (^{7}) in North London sorts some of them, and sends them to charity shops for (^{8}). That saves the environmental impact of making new clothes. But it's only a tiny (^{9}) of garments and shoes that get recycled. Most are (^{10}), with around 80% ending up in landfill, around 20% getting (^{11}).

25

Andrea Speranza, Campaign Manager, Textile Reuse and International Development (TRAID): The fashion industry is ranked four in term of

30

34

environmental impact, after housing and, er, food and transport. So that's give you an idea, the massive impact. The, er, the fashion industry, they, is an industry that poisons soil, pollutes, er, rivers, (^{12}) a lot of, massive amounts of carbon (^{13}).

Harrabin: And here's another recently (^{14}) problem. (^{15}) of synthetic fibres that are washed off our clothing. They're being eaten by creatures in the sea.

Harrabin: Working (^{16}) in the fashion industry are another concern for MPs. They've written to the chief executives of the UK's ten leading fashion retailers, to find out what they're doing to (^{17}) the environmental and social impact of the clothes and shoes they sell.

Andrew Opie, British Retail Consortium: We, as retailers, have a really res-, big responsibility making sure that those clothes are as (^{18}) as possible. And we know from the figures that we've been looking at, working with government, how we have cut things like energy and water use. There's much more we can do and that's what we've said in (^{19}) to this report.

Harrabin: The MPs welcome the move, but say there is a (^{20}) problem, with an industry that (^{21}) on people throwing away good clothes because they're last year's colour. They say fashion firms must try harder. Roger Harrabin, BBC News.

(Friday 5 October 2018)

Notes ··

l. 6: **The Commons Environmental Audit Committee**「庶民院環境監査委員会」政府の政策がどのように環境保護や持続可能な開発に貢献しているかを考察する下院の委員会　l. 14: **Mary Creagh**「メアリー・クレア（1967- ）」労働党議員。庶民院環境監査委員会の議長を務める　l. 30: **Textile Reuse and International Development (TRAID)**「織物再利用国際開発」衣服のリサイクルや資金集めによって環境を守り、世界の貧困を減らすことを目的とするイギリスの慈善団体　l. 34: **that's give you an idea** 文法的に正しくはthat's（＝that has）given you an ideaとなる　l. 47: **British Retail Consortium**「英国小売協会」イギリスの全小売業者のための商業組合

ロンドン・ファッション・ウィーク

　「ロンドン・ファッション・ウィーク（London Fashion Week）」は、毎年2月と9月に開催される高級服飾展示会で、250以上のデザイナーが集まり、ニューヨーク、ミラノ、パリと並んで「ビッグ・フォー（Big Four）」と呼ばれています。ロンドン・ファッション・ウィークの中心である「ロンドン・コレクション（London Collection）」は、1960年代にはモッズやミニスカート、1970年代にはパンクを流行させました。こうした若者文化発祥の伝統を保ちながら、老舗ブランドも健在で、活発なファッション発信の場となっています。1ヶ月前に開催される「ファッション・ウィーク・メンズ（Fashion Week Men's）」は、メンズファッションのマーケット拡大にも貢献しています。

▶▶▶ Moving On

6 Making a Summary

▌ Fill the gaps to complete the summary.

　World production of clothes has doubled in the last 15 years, and British people buy more than any other European nation. But when this clothing is (j　　　), very little gets (r　　　). Most of it is thrown away in landfill sites, with about 20% being (i　　　). Therefore, it (g　　　) carbon dioxide, which (f　　　) climate change. Also, soil and rivers are polluted, and (f　　　) of synthetic fibres are washed into the sea, where they are eaten by creatures. There is also concern about working conditions in the fashion industry. Because of this, British MPs have asked fashion retailers to explain how they will reduce this (m　　　) environmental and social (i　　　). The retailers accept that they have a responsibility to make the industry (s　　　), and are looking at cutting energy and water use. However, the MPs think they should try harder.

7 Follow Up

▌ Discuss, write or present.

1. Do you have a similar attitude to the women in the video, buying new clothes whenever there are new fashions, styles or colours, or do you keep your clothes for longer?

2. What happens to old clothes in Japan? Are they just incinerated, or put into landfill, or are they recycled?

3. How serious do you think the issues discussed in the unit are? What do you think retailers can do to make the fashion industry sustainable and protect the environment? What can we consumers do?

Community Cycling

イギリスで自転車と言えば、白人男性が乗るものと思われていますが、この度、マイノリティの人々も自転車に乗ることが奨励されつつあります。ニュースを見てみましょう。

▶ Starting Off

1 Setting the Scene

▌ What do you think?

1. What sort of things do you do to keep fit? Do you like to do them by yourself, or in the company of others?
2. Do you have a bicycle? How often do you use it, and why?
3. Is there anything that makes it difficult for you to ride a bicycle? What are the disadvantages of riding a bicycle?

2 Building Language

▌ Which word (1-6) best fits which explanation (a-f)?

1. perception   [   ]
2. under-represented   [   ]
3. funding   [   ]
4. convert   [   ]
5. access   [   ]
6. barrier   [   ]

a. ability, permission, or opportunity to use something
b. not counted or included enough
c. money provided towards a task, or the creation of something
d. something that obstructs or limits you
e. change or be changed into something different
f. the way that something is recognised and understood

3 Understanding Check 1

▌ Read the quotes, then watch the news and match them to the right people.

1. . . . so yeah, it, it is open to everyone.

   [　]

2. . . . because money is being spent to encourage Londoners from all backgrounds . . .　[　]

3. It's just free time for myself, and I've left the car at home.　[　]

4. . . . it's really easy for them to take up.　[　]

4 Understanding Check 2

▌ Which is the best answer?

1. What is the aim of the Hornbeam JoyRiders Club?
   a. to encourage under-represented groups to take up cycling
   b. to train cyclists of under-represented groups
   c. to help prevent discrimination among cyclists
   d. to create cycling courses for under-represented groups

2. How many people from black, Asian and minority ethnic backgrounds commuted once by bike?
   a. nobody
   b. fewer than half the number of people from white backgrounds who commuted once by bike
   c. twice the number of people from white backgrounds who commuted once by bike
   d. nearly everybody

3. The women talked about what they liked about the club. Which of the following was <u>not</u> mentioned?
   a. They can check out cafés.
   b. They can socialise and network with other women.
   c. They can save money.
   d. They have freedom to go to places.

▌What do you remember?

4. What is the perception that some people have of cycling commuters?

_____

5. Some people don't have a bike, so how can they ride with the JoyRiders?

_____

6. According to the last woman, what is it that makes women think that they can cycle themselves?

_____

●●Background Information●●

　健康的で環境にやさしい移動手段として近年注目されている自転車ですが、実は、誰もが気軽に利用できるものというわけではありません。ロンドン大学衛生熱帯医学大学院（the London School of Hygiene and Tropical Medicine）は2008年10月から1年間、様々な民族性や文化的背景、職業などを持つ78人の男女を対象とし、ロンドンでの自転車の利用に関する聞き取り調査を行いました。その結果、多くの人が、自転車に乗っている人は生活に余裕のある白人男性であり、サイクリングは社会的地位や意識の高さを反映している、と考えていることがわかりました。自転車を利用することに引け目を感じている人も少なくなく、特に、今回のニュースにも登場していたイスラム系の女性たちは、宗教令であるファトワー（fatwa）によって公共の場で自転車に乗ることを禁止されており、気軽にサイクリングを楽しみづらいのが現状です。

　ロンドン市では、2013年に当時の市長だったボリス・ジョンソン（Boris Johnson, 1964- ）が掲げた「ロンドンでのサイクリングに向けての市長の展望（The Mayor's Vision for Cycling in London)」以降、自転車の積極的な利用を推奨してきました。より広範囲の人々に自転車の利用を普及させるべく、ロンドン交通局（Transport for London）では2015年以来、「サイクリング・グランツ・ロンドン（Cycling Grants London）」という助成金を導入しています。申請が認められた団体は、3年間で最高1万ポンドまでの補助を受けることができ、自転車や整備工具の購入、初心者へのトレーニングなど、より多くの人に自転車に乗ってもらうための様々な活動に資金を充てることができます。こうした動きの中、2018年、ロンドン市長サディク・カーン（Sadiq Khan, 1970- ）は「市長の交通戦略（The Mayor's Transport Strategy）」を発表し、自転車や徒歩、公共交通機関による移動を2041年までに全体の80%に増やすことを目標として掲げました。これにより、ロンドン交通網の改善と混雑の解消を図ると同時に、自動車の利用が引き起こしている深刻な大気汚染を減少させ、市民の健康を促進することを目指しています。誰もが自転車を楽しみ健康な生活を送ることができる街の実現に向け、多くの人々が動いています。

参考：https://www.theguardian.com/uk-news/davehillblog/2015/oct/12/why-are-london-cyclists-so-white-male-and-middle-class

https://www.cyclinggrants.london/

5 Filling Gaps　　News Story

▌ Watch the News, then fill the gaps in the text.

Newsreader: Now, er, a question for you. When I say "cycling commuters", do middle-aged men in Lycra (^{1}　　　　) to mind? Well, rightly or wrongly, that does seem to be the (^{2}　　　　) by some. So hold that thought because money is being spent to encourage Londoners from all backgrounds, to get on their bikes. Here's our transport correspondent, Tom Edwards.

Tom Edwards: Meet Hornbeam JoyRiders Club in Waltham Forest. It's been going for two years. And it aims to encourage women and other (^{3}　　　　　　) groups to take up cycling. Its training courses have been a huge (^{4}　　　　　). Attiya Khan is a GP. She's been with the group since September.

Attiya Khan: For me, this was (^{5}　　　　　) because it was, it was, it's just a, in a different group of women. You know, and just, you know Muslim women, people from different backgrounds, so all (^{6}　　　　　), so yeah, it, it is open to everyone.

Edwards: The Mayor today gave (^{7}　　　　　) to 30 more groups like this, to encourage Londoners from all backgrounds to cycle. And safe (^{8}　　　　　) is also important.

First woman: After finding the group, it's like I (^{9}　　　　　) with other women, network, networking, checking out the cafés. It's just free time for myself, and I've left the car at home.

Second woman: Yes, I've (^{10}　　　　　) (*laughs*). I love cycling. I, er, it's, it's, as I say before, that's, it's give freedom for me to go anywhere instead of walking.

Edwards: The latest TfL figures show that in one year, just 15% of people from black, Asian and minority (^{11}　　　　　) backgrounds (^{12}　　　　　) once by bike. That (^{13}　　　　　) to 40% of people from white backgrounds, but it is

changing.

Third woman: People, if they don't know anyone else like themselves cycling, um, then they're less likely to cycle 'cos they just don't think it's for them. And obviously (^{14}) to a bike is a big (^{15}) as well. A lot of people don't have a bike or they don't have anywhere to store a bike. So, just the fact that we can, um, invite people on led bike rides, and offer them a bike, it's really easy for them to take up.

Fourth woman: What you need to do is create community (^{16}) from different groups. And so the Hornbeam JoyRiders here, um, in Leyton have been working with women from Muslim backgrounds, different (^{17}) minority communities. Once you see other people like yourself doing it, once you see more women cycling, I think, er, there is a, er, a desire then to think, well, actually I can do this myself.

Edwards: The Mayor has big (^{18}) to get more people cycling. One battle will be (^{19}) those who don't think cycling is for them. Tom Edwards, BBC London News.

(Tuesday 22 January 2019)

Notes ··

l. 3: **Lycra**「ライクラ」1959年にアメリカのデュポン社が開発したポリウレタン繊維。伸縮性があり、動きやすいため、スキーや自転車などのスポーツウェアに用いられる　l. 10: **Hornbeam JoyRiders Club**「ホーンビーム・ジョイライダーズ・クラブ」2017年1月に結成された、サイクリングを通じて少数派の女性などを支援する団体。Hornbeamは長距離レースで活躍したイギリスのサラブレッド競走馬（1953-77）の名前に由来する　l. 10: **Waltham Forest**「ウォルサム・フォレスト」ロンドン北東部に位置するロンドン自治区　l. 13: **GP (＝general practitioner)**「総合診療医」患者の生活に着目し、全体的な健康問題に向き合って治療を行う医師。イギリス国民はNHS（国民保健サービス）の医療を受けるために、GP登録を行うことが義務づけられている　l. 27: **TfL (＝Transport for London)**「ロンドン交通局」大ロンドンの公共交通事業を管理する行政機関。交通政策の実行と公共交通システムの運営を業務とする　l. 43: **Leyton**「レイトン」ウォルサム・フォレストにある町

女性の解放と自転車

1918年2月6日、イギリスで女性の投票権が認められ、その1世紀後のケンブリッジ大学で、女性参政権運動を描いた当時のポスターの展覧会が開催されました。その中には、自転車に乗る女性を描いたものもあります。実際自転車に乗ることは、女性の解放と強く結びついていました。アメリカのアニー・コーエン・コプチョフスキー（Annie Cohen Kopchovsky, 1870-1947）は、1万ドルを賭け、家族をボストンに残し、船と自転車で世界一周を果たし、途中日本に寄っています。幕末から明治の横浜や築地の外国人居留地でも、いち早く自転車を取り入れた音楽学校の女学生や芸者の姿を、『ジャパン・パンチ（Japan Punch)』のチャールズ・ワーグマン（Charles Wirgman, 1832-91）や『トバエ（TÔBAÉ)』のジョルジュ・ビゴー（Georges Bigot, 1860-1927）が描きました。

▶▶▶ Moving On

6 Making a Summary

CD1-22

Fill the gaps to complete the summary.

Many people have the (p   ) that only middle-aged white men commute on bicycles. That is not far from the truth, as in fact, only 15% of people from non-white (e   ) (b   ) commute even only once a year by bike. Because of this, the Mayor has provided (f   ) to create clubs aiming to encourage women and other (u   ) groups to take up cycling. One such group, the Hornbeam JoyRiders, is very successful. It includes people from different (b   ), including Muslim women. Many of them say they (c   ) to cycling when they saw other people like themselves doing it. They say they can socialise, network, check out cafés, and have their own freedom to go places. One (b   ) is that they sometimes don't have (a   ) to a bike of their own, but the club offers them bikes to use.

7 Follow Up

Discuss, write or present.

1. Why do you think the Mayor wants to encourage cycling? Do you think that it is a good way to spend tax money?

2. How many people commute by bicycle where you live? Would you like to cycle more than you do at the moment? Do you think a club like the Hornbeam JoyRiders would encourage you?

3. Do you think it is better to do things together rather than by yourself? What are the advantages of clubs like this? What clubs have you belonged to?

Unit **8**
A Smartphone Amnesty

近年、スマートフォンに依存する人が増える中、スマホのない生活に挑戦しているティーンエイジャーたちがいます。スマホ世代に向けた取り組みについて、ニュースを見てみましょう。

▶ **Starting Off**

1 Setting the Scene

▌ **What do you think?**

1. Did you have a mobile phone when you were at junior high school? Why do you think that so many young school pupils have mobile phones?
2. What effects (good or bad) do you think mobile phones have on pupils?
3. What was your school's policy about using mobile phones? What about other schools that you know about? Do you agree with these policies?

2 Building Language

▌ **Which word (1-6) best fits which explanation (a-f)?**

1. curb   [   ]   **a.** strength; the ability to stay strong
2. ban   [   ]   **b.** the pleasing feeling of being satisfied
3. subsidise   [   ]   **c.** control something by reducing its frequency
4. murky   [   ]   **d.** dark and gloomy; obscure and hard to understand
5. resilience   [   ]   **e.** pay money to help reduce the cost of something
6. gratification [   ]   **f.** prohibit the sale or use of something

3 Understanding Check 1

▌ Read the quotes, then watch the news and match them to the right people.

1. But as time goes on, you'd want to reintroduce that, and give them the skills to moderate themselves . . . [   ]

2. . . . they don't want their child to give up their phone completely . . .   [   ]

3. Different schools in London have different policies when it comes to their pupils and their mobile phones. [   ]

4. . . . although I may have, um, short-term pain, it's for the long-term gain.
                                [   ]

4 Understanding Check 2

▌ Which is the best answer?

1. What sort of amnesty has the Michaela Community School called for?
   a. Mobile phones must be turned off during class time.
   b. Pupils give up their smartphones, but can buy a cheap basic phone.
   c. Mobile phones are banned from the school grounds.
   d. Pupils must not spend hours on the internet.

2. By how much does the school subsidise the sale of basic phones?
   a. £4
   b. £7
   c. £10
   d. £14

3. The students talked about the benefits of this amnesty. Which of the following did they not mention?
   a. They will think more about their homework.
   b. They can spend more time with their family.
   c. They don't have to worry about their online image.
   d. They will be able to communicate more with their friends.

4. According to this news story, what is the 'iGeneration'?

_____

5. Why do parents love the basic phones that the pupils can buy?

_____

6. Why do many mental health professionals welcome this amnesty?

_____

●●Background Information●●

　1990年代よりインターネットや携帯電話が普及し、2007年のiPhoneの発売により電話とネットが一体化して以来、スマホは人々の生活に深く入り込んできました。便利な一方で、中毒性や心身に与える悪影響が懸念されるようになっています。特に、物心ついて以来、スマホを常に身近なものとして育った子供や若者世代への影響が心配されています。イギリスでガイドラインが出されたのと同じ頃、アメリカでも過去最大規模の研究結果が発表され、スクリーンを見ている時間の長い子供ほど、脳の形状に変化が見られるということが明らかになりました。

　2018年9月、就任間もないマット・ハンコック（Matt Hancock, 1978- ）保健・社会福祉相は、政府主席医務官デイム・サリー・デイヴィス（Dame Sally Davies, 1949- ）に、子供がSNSに接する時間を制限するガイドラインを作成するよう依頼しました。しかしながら、SNSやスマホ、ネットなどの線引きや、具体的な数字での制限は難しく、心身への影響も、良いものと悪いものの程度や区別が付きにくいため、様々な研究における分析結果も分かれています。

　また、SNSの青少年に有害なコンテンツについても、問題視する声が大きくなってきています。2017年11月に当時14歳だったモリー・ラッセルという少女がインスタグラムで自傷行為や自殺関連の投稿を閲覧した後自殺するという出来事があり、彼女の父親は死の責任の一端はソーシャルメディアを運営する企業にあると述べました。その訴えを受け、ハンコック相は、SNSの運営会社がコンテンツ対策を強化しない場合、国内でブロッキングする可能性についても語り、各運営会社も対策を打つよう求められています。

　ニュースで言及されている2019年2月に発行されたガイドラインでは、少なくとも2時間に1度は休憩を取ることや、就寝前には使用を避けることなどを規定しているものの、具体的な時間数の制限などは設けられませんでした。しかし、SNSやスマホを子供や若者が利用する時の内容や量に関して、注意を払う必要があることは間違いありません。

参考：https://www.wired.co.uk/article/social-media-guidelines-matt-hancock

　　　https://www.theguardian.com/technology/2018/jan/27/mobile-phone-addiction-apps-break-the-habit-take-back-control

　　　https://bigthink.com/mind-brain/screen-time-nih-study-60-minutes

▌**Watch the news, then fill the gaps in the text.**

Newsreader: On the day the government has published guidelines on (^{1}) children's smartphone use, one London school has gone a step further by calling for an amnesty. Some pupils at the Michaela Community School, in Wembley, have handed in their smartphones for six months, with teachers providing discounted 'brick phones', that are not (^{2}) to the internet. Sarah Harris reports.

Sarah Harris: It's become known as the 'iGeneration': teenagers spending hours on their phones, rather than (^{3}) (^{4}) the world around them. It's a (^{5}) for parents and teachers alike.

Harris: Different schools in London have different policies when it comes to their pupils and their mobile phones. Some insist that they're (^{6}) (^{7}) during class time, others (^{8}) them from the school grounds. But this school have taken it one step further.

First student: Miss, can I hand in my phone?

Harris: Here, at the Michaela Community School in Wembley, they're holding a smartphone amnesty, some agreeing to give up their (^{9}) for six months.

Teacher: Maybe next time we'll think about keeping it until the end of your exams.

First student: I believe that although I may have, um, short-term pain, it's for the long-term gain.

Second student: It's also allowed me to get a (^{10}) (^{11}) (^{12}), and spend more time with my family, because I'm not (^{13}) worried about putting up this perfect image online, on the internet.

Third student: When you get likes, it will give you a (^{14}), and when you hear that, you'll start reflecting on that, rather than reflecting on your homework.

Harris: The school does offer basic phones at a (^{15}) price, to encourage a move away from the 24/7 internet.

Katharine Birbalsingh, Headteacher of Michaela Community School: We sell these phones, at school, for £10. We, we buy them for 14, we sell them (^{16}), for £10. Er, and the reason is because parents love the (^{17}). Er, they don't want their child to give up their phone completely, because they want to be able to get in touch with their child. You can text them, you can ring them with a brick phone, but what it doesn't allow your child to do, is get involved in the (^{18}) and (^{19}) world of Snapchat and Instagram.

Fourth student: These days, children are getting bullied and abused . . .

Harris: These students are leading the way. Now, classes are being (^{20}) to parents who want a family iPhone detox too. Many mental health professionals welcome the time out as a first step.

Stefan Walter, addiction therapist: It's giving those children an experience of not having their phones at their side all the time, and they're going to have to get used to that, and build up some (^{21}) to be bored sometimes, and to feel frustrated sometimes, and not to have that instant (^{22}) that the phone normally offers. So, it's a good start. But as time goes on, you'd want to reintroduce that, and give them the skills to moderate themselves, to learn to (^{23}).

Harris: It will be a hard sell for some teenagers to give up the (^{24}) and high-tech world of the internet on their phones. But these students say it's simply made their lives better. Sarah Harris, BBC London News.

(Thursday 7 February 2019)

Notes ··

l. 5: **amnesty**「猶予」本来は、政治犯などに対する恩赦や減刑を意味する　l. 6: **the Michaela Community School**「ミカエラ・コミュニティ・スクール」ロンドンにあるフリースクール。2014年開校　l. 7: **Wembley**「ウェンブリー」ロンドン北西部の地区　l. 8: **brick phones**「ブリックフォン」1980年代に市販されるようになった、初期の携帯電話の愛称。レンガ（brick）のように大きく重いことからそう呼ばれた。ここでは、インターネット等の多機能を搭載せず、通話機能を主とする携帯電話のことを指している　l. 33: **basic phones**「ベーシックフォン」brick phonesの言い換え。通話等の最低限の機能のみを搭載した携帯電話のこと　l. 47: **iPhone detox**「iPhoneデトックス」detoxは体内から有害物質を取り除く過程やその期間を意味し、しばしば麻薬やアルコール依存症などに対する治療法を指す。ここでは、iPhone等のスマートフォンに依存した生活から抜け出すことを表している

イギリスの携帯電話会社

イギリスの携帯電話には大手5社があり、それぞれ特徴があります。Vodafone（ボーダフォン）はヨーロッパでのシェアが1位で繋がりやすく、O₂（オー・ツー）はBT（British Telecom）のモバイル事業部を前身としており固定電話と連動しています。3（スリー）はプランが一番安くて人気、ドイツ系のT-Mobile（Tモバイル）は東ヨーロッパとロシアで強く、フランス系のOrange（オレンジ）は海外で使用できる国が多い上、イギリス国内でも強いネットワークを持っています。

▶▶▶ Moving On

6 Making a Summary

CD1-25

▌ Fill the gaps to complete the summary.

The government is trying to (c   ) children's smartphone use, because if they spend hours on phones, they might not (e   ) (i   ) the world around them. Some schools (b   ) mobile phones, but the Michaela School has called for an (a   ). Pupils can hand in their smartphones for six months, and instead purchase a basic mobile phone that is not connected to the internet. They cost only £10 because the school (s   ) them by £4 each. Pupils are happy because they can think about homework instead of likes. They are not (c   ) worried about their online image, and get better sleep. Parents like the basic phones because they can keep in touch with their children, who are no longer involved in the (m   ) world of the internet. Mental health specialists believe that it is good that children don't have instant (g   ) all the time. They can build up (r   ) to being bored and frustrated.

7 Follow Up

▌ Discuss, write or present.

1. Do you think the Michaela Community School's smartphone amnesty is a good idea? Would Japanese pupils welcome it in the same way?

2. The addiction therapist says that it is good for students not to have 'instant gratification', so they can build more resilience to being bored and frustrated. Do you agree? Are there any other examples of modern 'instant gratification'?

3. Read about the Michaela Community School on the internet. The school emphasises discipline and there is a "zero tolerance" policy towards bad behaviour. What do you think of such policies? Are they different from policies in Japanese schools?

Unit 9
Guide Dog Discrimination

ロンドンのとあるレストランで盲導犬を連れた男性が入店を拒否されました。彼はどのように感じているのでしょうか。ニュースを見てみましょう。

▶ Starting Off

1 Setting the Scene

▌ What do you think?

1. Do you have a dog, or do you know somebody who has a dog? Why do you think people have dogs?
2. Can dogs be useful? Think of ways in which dogs can help humans.
3. On the other hand, can dogs cause problems? What sort of problems might they cause?

2 Building Language

▌ For each word (1-6), find two synonyms (a-l).

1. humiliated   [/   ]
2. rejected   [/   ]
3. dejected   [/   ]
4. stance   [/   ]
5. discriminatory   [/   ]
6. stigma   [/   ]

a. discouraged   **g.** disgrace
b. shame   **h.** attitude
c. alone   **i.** depressed
d. abandoned   **j.** viewpoint
e. disgraced   **k.** unfair
f. biased   **l.** embarrassed

49

③ Understanding Check 1

▌ Read the quotes, then watch the news and match them to the right people.

1. ... and that's any dog, let alone an assistance dog. [ ]

2. All I wanted to do was do what hundreds of thousands of Londoners do every day ... [ ]

3. And he's so fed up with it, he's now taking legal action. [ ]

4. It was here on Tottenham Court Road at this branch ... [ ]

④ Understanding Check 2

▌ Which is the best answer?

1. How did Dave Kent feel when he was not allowed to take his guide dog into the restaurant?
   a. He felt happy.
   b. He felt human.
   c. He felt humiliated.
   d. He felt horrible.

2. What happened when Dave was in the restaurant?
   a. The restaurant asked him for the dog's paperwork, but he couldn't find it.
   b. He ordered a nice lunch, but they couldn't hear him.
   c. The restaurant told him to leave because his paperwork was not legal.
   d. He showed them the dog's paperwork, but they told him to leave anyway.

3. What finally happened?
   a. The restaurant refused to apologise, because dogs are not allowed in restaurants.
   b. The restaurant admitted that its staff had made a mistake.
   c. The restaurant is considering legal action.
   d. The restaurant paid for his lunch at a different restaurant.

What do you remember?

4. What is Dave's stance about what happened?

_____

5. Why did the owner of the restaurants invite Dave to lunch?

_____

6. What is the law about dogs in restaurants?

_____

●●Background Information●●

　イギリスでは約36万人が全盲または弱視の視覚障害者として登録されており、約5,000人が盲導犬を利用しています。白杖やGPSと同様、盲導犬は視覚障害者の移動を支える重要な手段であり、日常生活を送る上での大切なパートナーです。

　2010年に制定された平等法（the Equality Act）は、視覚障害者を含む全ての障害者の権利を保障し、障害を理由とする不当な差別を禁じています。商店、銀行、ホテル、パブ、レストランといったあらゆる施設において、視覚障害を持つ人は障害のない人と同等のサービスを受けることができ、サービスの提供者は、障害者に不利益が生じないよう「合理的調整（reasonable adjustment）」を行うことが義務づけられています。盲導犬を提供している慈善団体「ガイド・ドッグズ（Guide Dogs）」や盲導犬・介助犬関連の慈善団体の合同組織「アシスタンス・ドッグズUK（Assistance Dogs UK）」によると、盲導犬や介助犬を同伴している場合でも、視覚障害者の権利は同様に保障されます。例えば飲食店では、メニューの音読または点字で書かれたメニュー表の提供や、会計時の介助、セルフサービス形式の店での介助の申し出等の、柔軟な対応が求められます。また、これらの対応に加えて、盲導犬や介助犬を同伴している人に対しては、入店を受け入れることはもちろん、テーブルの下に犬が伏せることのできる十分なスペースのある座席を提供することなどが必要とされています。

　今回のニュースで取り上げられていたレストランの対応は、平等法で定められているこうした障害者への配慮に欠けたものでしたが、一方で、衛生上の問題や宗教を理由として犬の入店を拒否する店はいまだ少なくなく、盲導犬や介助犬同伴での入店を断られる事例がイギリス各地で度々報告されています。

参考：https://www.guidedogs.org.uk/media/5350/food-premises-access-guide.pdf#search=%27uk+guide+dog+restaurant%27

http://www.assistancedogs.org.uk/law/

5 Filling Gaps   News Story

CD2-02 [Original]   CD2-03 [Voiced]

Watch the news, then fill the gaps in the text.

Newsreader: A blind man says he feels (¹   ) after he was told he couldn't eat at a restaurant in central London because he was with his guide dog. Dave Kent says he and fellow guide dog owners are now increasingly experiencing (²   ) in London. And he's so fed up with it, he's now taking legal action. Victoria Cook has been speaking to him.

5

Dave Kent, Guide Dogs Mobility Team (*to his dog*): Forward, Chad. Come on, son. What is it?

10

Victoria Cook: This is Chad and Dave.

Kent (*to his dog*): Where you going, Chaddie?

Cook: Together, they enjoy coming into London for lunch. That was until last week, when a restaurant (³   ) to let them in. Staff said, "No dogs allowed."

15

Kent: All I wanted to do was do what hundreds of thousands of Londoners do every day, which is to go and enjoy a nice lunch. I couldn't do that, which left me, um, feeling, er, (⁴   ), (⁵   ) and utterly (⁶   ).

Cook: It was here on Tottenham Court Road at this branch of Franco Manca where it happened. Dave said he showed staff paperwork which shows the dog is (⁷   ) allowed to be inside, but they wouldn't listen.

20

Cook: Dave works with the guide dogs and has had his own for 40 years. He says he's seen (⁸   ) of the laws about them getting worse, and he's had enough.

25

Kent: My (⁹   ) is to, er, to speak for those who aren't so, um, (¹⁰   ) and the people who're (¹¹   ) every day of their, their lives, um, by people who behave in a (¹²   ) manner.

30

Cook: Today, Dave and Chad have been invited to have lunch in Bank. The owner here says he heard what happened and wanted to make up for it (^{13}) (^{14}) (^{15}) the restaurant industry.

35

Martin Williams, founder of M Restaurants: I think there's a (^{16}) against animals in restaurants. There's no law about dogs not being allowed in restaurants, and that's any dog, let alone an assistance dog. So, um, it's 40 quite an odd, um, situation where the industry's so (^{17}) in their thinking.

Cook: Franco Manca has issued an (^{18}) and said it was a mistake made by staff here. It's now (^{19}) training to stop this from happening in the future. Despite the (^{20}), Dave says he's now 45 considering legal action against the restaurant. He wants the industry to be more welcoming to those with assistance dogs. Victoria Cook, BBC London News.

(Sunday 10 June 2018)

Notes ···

l. 10: **Guide Dogs Mobility Team**「盲導犬歩行チーム」盲導犬の育成を行う慈善団体。イギリスの主要な各都市に存在する　l. 20: **Tottenham Court Road**「トテナム・コート・ロード」ロンドン中心のフィッツロヴィア地区の主要な道路　l. 20: **Franco Manca**「フランコ・マンカ」イギリスとイタリアに40店舗以上あるチェーン店のピザレストラン。2008年創業　l. 33: **Bank**「バンク」イングランド銀行（the Bank of England）があるロンドンの中心地　l. 38: **M Restaurants**「Mレストラン」ロンドンを中心に数店舗あるステーキレストラン。2014年創業

イギリス児童文学と犬

日本でアニメ化されて人気を博した『フランダースの犬』（*A Dog of Flanders*, 1872）は、イギリスの児童文学作家ウィーダ（Ouida: Marie Louise de la Ramée, 1839-1908）によって書かれ、貧しい少年ネロと愛犬パトラッシュの友情を描いた悲劇として知られています。ウィーダは犬好きで、動物愛護に尽力しましたが、晩年はペットの飼育費が生活費を圧迫し、困窮を極めました。J・M・バリー（James Matthew Barrie, 1860-1937）の創作した妖精ピーターパン（Peter Pan）を主人公とする物語に登場する犬のナナは、子供たちの世話を完璧にこなす乳母です。ナナの犬種は、バリー夫妻が異なる時期に飼っていたニューファウンドランド犬とセント・バーナード犬の両方の影響を受けているようです。

▶▶▶ Moving On

6 Making a Summary

CD2-04

▌Fill the gaps to complete the summary.

Dave Kent, who is blind, felt (h⎯⎯⎯⎯⎯⎯) when he had to leave the Franco Manca restaurant because they told him that his guide dog, Chad, was not allowed in. They wouldn't listen even when he showed them the dog's paperwork. He felt (r⎯⎯⎯⎯) and (d⎯⎯⎯⎯⎯⎯). He has had a dog for 40 years, and says (i⎯⎯⎯⎯⎯) of the laws is getting worse, with many people acting in a (d⎯⎯⎯⎯⎯⎯⎯) manner. He was invited to lunch by Martin Williams, the founder of an expensive restaurant chain, who wanted to make up for Mr. Kent's bad experience on (b⎯⎯⎯⎯⎯) of the restaurant industry. Mr. Williams said that his industry's thinking is backwards, and even though there is no law about dogs in restaurants, there is still a (s⎯⎯⎯⎯⎯) against them. Franco Manca have apologised. However, Mr. Kent might take legal action. His (s⎯⎯⎯⎯⎯) is to speak for people who aren't so confident in such situations as he is.

7 Follow Up

▌Discuss, write or present.

1. How do you feel about dogs in restaurants? Should they be allowed or not? Should there be special rules for guide dogs like Chad?

2. Mr. Kent is considering legal action, so the restaurant might be punished. Do you think this is the best thing to do? Is there anything else he could do about it?

3. Have a look at the website at https://www.guidedogs.org.uk. What do you think of this organisation? Is there a similar one in Japan? Many people who work with guide dogs are volunteers. Why do you think they volunteer?

Unit 10
Financial Literacy at School

イギリスの地方都市のとある学校に、ロンドンから中央銀行の首席エコノミストが授業をしにやって来ました。一体、どのような授業なのでしょうか。ニュースを見てみましょう。

▶ Starting Off

1 Setting the Scene

▌ What do you think?

1. When we talk about 'the economy', what do you think we mean by that?
2. Are you 'good with money'? In other words, do you spend money responsibly, or not?
3. What important financial decisions have you had to make, or will have to make in the future? Do you think you are good at making financial decisions?

2 Building Language

▌ Which word (1-6) best fits which explanation (a-f)?

1. equip   [   ]   **a.** a long way away; unrelated
2. crucial   [   ]   **b.** the largest, most important part of something
3. extortionate   [   ]   **c.** very expensive; almost impossible to afford
4. struggle   [   ]   **d.** very important indeed
5. remote   [   ]   **e.** prepare somebody and give them what they need
6. mainstream   [   ]   **f.** find it difficult to succeed or survive

3 Understanding Check 1

▌ Read the quotes, then watch the news and match them to the right people.

1. ... you have to focus on what house you're going to buy ...   [　]

2. ... perhaps even a compulsory part of the curriculum.   [　]

3. Financial literacy should be part of the national curriculum.   [　]

4. ... unfortunately they may end up going to, you know, the shop in, in the local town centre ...   [　]

4 Understanding Check 2

▌ Which is the best answer?

1. According to the Chief Economist of the Bank of England, what could financial literacy help us to prevent?
   a. unemployment
   b. ill health
   c. getting into debt
   d. inflation

2. The students were asked about what the economy meant to them. Which of the following was not an answer?
   a. It's about your future and what is going on around you.
   b. It's about building successful companies and making money.
   c. It's about being able to buy food and warmth.
   d. It's about borrowing money and going to banks.

3. According to the Headteacher, why are parents going to shops that charge extortionate rates?
   a. They need to borrow money to pay bills and buy school equipment.
   b. They want to buy fashionable top-brand clothes.
   c. They want a mortgage to buy a house.
   d. They need to buy good food for the family.

What do you remember?

4. Why does the Chief Economist of the Bank of England want to change the national curriculum?

_____

5. According to the Chief Economist, what can affect the whole of people's lives?

_____

6. For many people, what is wrong with the Bank of England?

_____

●●Background Information●●

　今回のニュースが放送された2018年4月、イングランド銀行は「エコノME（econoME）」という学習教材の無料配布をウェブサイト上で開始しました。経済が自分や周囲の人々の生活にどのような影響を与えているかを知り、お金に関する適切な選択や意思決定を下す力を身に付けるための教材で、11歳から16歳の生徒を対象としています。学習内容は、①経済的要因が個人のお金に関する決定にどのような影響を与えるか、②どのように情報を整理し適切な決定を下すか、③その決定が、自分自身や周囲の人々、そして経済そのものにどのような結果をもたらすか、の3部構成となっており、経済を身近なものとしてとらえ、体系的に学べるよう工夫されています。

　実際、金融リテラシー教育の拡充は、借金を抱える人が増加しつつあるイギリスにおいては切実な課題です。2017年、イギリスの各世帯における年間の支出額が、過去30年間で初めて収入額を上回りました。収入に対する支出の不足金額は年間平均900ポンド（約12万円）で、その大半が借金によって補填されていました。また、2018年6月時点での各世帯における住宅ローン等を含む借金の平均金額は58,540ポンド（約810万円）で、人口全体では1.6兆ポンド（約224兆円）となり、前年の1.5兆ポンドから増加しました。物価の高騰や賃金の低下によって世帯収入が減少する中、より貧しい世帯ほど、日々の生活を賄うために借金をし、貯蓄を切り崩しているのが現状です。特に、高利で少額からお金を借りることができるペイデイ・ローン（payday loan）を使って気軽に借金をする人が多いことも問題となっています。子供のうちから経済を身近なものとして学び、身の丈に合った、お金の適切な使い方を身に付けることが求められています。

参考：https://www.bankofengland.co.uk/education/econome

　　　https://www.ons.gov.uk/economy/nationalaccounts/uksectoraccounts/articles/makingendsmeetarehouseholds
　　　livingbeyondtheirmeans/2018-07-26

　　　https://theconversation.com/generation-debt-uk-below-average-at-teaching-financial-literacy-90326

5 Filling Gaps   News Story

CD2-05 [Original]   CD2-06 [Voiced]

❚ Watch the news, then fill the gaps in the text.

Newsreader: Financial literacy should be part of the national curriculum. That's according to the Chief Economist of the Bank of England. In a BBC interview, Andy Haldane said it could help (¹   ) people getting into (²   ). Well, our education editor, Branwen Jeffreys, joined him at a school, to find out how much teenagers understand about the economy.   5

Andy Haldane, Chief Economist at the Bank of England: We talk about the   10 economy. What do you think we mean by that?

Branwen Jeffreys: It's a long way from the Bank of England, but their top economist is (³   ) to hear from these teenagers. We took him to Kirkby, on Merseyside.

Haldane: Let's go here.   15

First student: Is it inflation?

Haldane: It's inflation! Exactly.

Jeffreys: He thinks they should learn more about money. The bank says it wants to help schools, (⁴   ) plans for lessons on the economy, (⁵   ) pupils better for adult life.   20

Haldane: The (⁶   ) of poor financial decision-making, say, (⁷   ) the whole of people's lives. Understanding those (⁸   ) choices about finances or about jobs that are so (⁹   ), we know, to people's life chances. More of that, I think, needs to be in the (¹⁰   ) of the curriculum, perhaps even a   25 compulsory part of the curriculum.

Jeffreys: He heard from the Headteacher they already teach some money (¹¹   ). So, what does the economy mean to these teenagers?   30

Second student: The economy is, you know,

it's origin, your future. And erm, what's going on around you.

Third student: Being able to pay for warmth, erm, and buy food.

Fourth student: To borrow money, you could even go to a bank, or to a provident, er, service.

Fifth student: Well, when you grow up, you have to focus on what house you're going to buy and how much your mortgage is going to be.

Tony McGuiness, Headteacher of All Saints Catholic High School (*quietly in background*): My job as Headteacher is to make sure that . . .

Jeffreys: I heard families in Kirkby face tough choices. When there's a financial (^{12}), credit isn't always cheap.

McGuiness: For some of our parents and carers, you know, the (^{13}) is on. Er, we need some money tomorrow to pay our (^{14}), to make sure our children have got the (^{15}) to go to school. And so, unfortunately they may end up going to, you know, the shop in, in the local town centre that's charging (^{16}) rates.

Haldane (*quietly in background*): And helping you manage your money . . .

Jeffreys: The bank's top economist wants them to listen more to places like Kirkby. Families in work, who feel like they're (^{17}), high cost credit on offer on the high street. But for many, the Bank of England will feel (^{18}), the economy of the South East a million miles away, something no school lessons can (^{19}). Branwen Jeffreys, BBC News.

(*Friday 27 April 2018*)

Notes ···

l. 3: **the Bank of England**「イングランド銀行」イギリスの中央銀行。1694年設立　l. 14: **Kirkby**「カービー」イングランドの北西、マージーサイドに位置する都市　l. 14: **Merseyside**「マージーサイド」イングランド北西部の州。リヴァプールを中心都市とする　l. 37: **provident service**「積立サービス」provident fund（退職金積立基金）の言い間違いと思われる　l. 41: **All Saints Catholic High School**「オール・セインツ・カトリック高校」マージーサイド州カービーにある11歳から18歳の生徒が通うカトリックの中等学校

▶▶▶ Moving On

6 Making a Summary

Fill the gaps to complete the summary.

In poorer parts of Britain, like Kirkby, on Merseyside, people are (s _____) financially. In order to pay bills, they often make poor financial decisions and borrow money at shops that lend at (e _____) interest rates. Poor decision-making can affect people all their lives. Because of this, the Bank of England wants financial literacy to be in the (m _____) of the school curriculum. This would (e _____) students to understand (t _____), but (c _____) choices about finances. Students at a school in Kirkby were asked what the economy meant to them, and they mentioned paying for food, buying a house with a (m _____) and borrowing money. However, perhaps school lessons cannot fix the fact that the Bank of England seems (r _____), in London, a far richer part of the country.

7 Follow Up

Discuss, write or present.

1. Do you agree that 'financial literacy' should be part of the school curriculum? Do you think that you learnt (or are learning) enough at school to help you make wise financial decisions?

2. The Headteacher mentioned the problem of poor people having to borrow money at extortionate rates. Is this also a problem in Japan? What can be done about it?

3. With a partner, write a list of important financial decisions that people have to make in their lives. Which ones are the most difficult to make, and why? What financial decisions have you made? How difficult were they?

巨匠レオナルド・ダ・ヴィンチの作品を巡って、ヨーロッパである騒動が起きています。芸術の枠を超えて複雑な様相を呈するこの問題について、ニュースを見てみましょう。

▶ Starting Off

1 Setting the Scene

▌ What do you think?

1. How many European artists do you know about? With a partner, write a list. What are their most important works?
2. From the list you have written, who do you think is the most important artist, and why?
3. Describe to a partner an art museum that you have been to. What kind of art did it contain, and by which artists? Did you find it interesting?

2 Building Language

▌ Which word (1-5) best fits which explanation (a-e)?

1. spat   [   ]   **a.** delicate; easily broken or damaged
2. custody   [   ]   **b.** form the first idea of something
3. fragile   [   ]   **c.** keeping; looking after; guarding something
4. revelation   [   ]   **d.** a quarrel about a small thing that appears unimportant
5. conceive   [   ]   **e.** something found out in a surprising way

3 Understanding Check 1

▎ Read the quotes, then watch the news and match them to the right people.

1. But that's not how this argument is playing out.   [   ]

2. Yes, Leonardo is Italian.   [   ]

3. Now, do you recognise this painting?   [   ]

4. . . . there are very, very sophisticated, er, ways of having paintings, er, travel nowadays.   [   ]

4 Understanding Check 2

▎ Which is the best answer?

1. What is the spat about?
   a. Italy wants France to return the Mona Lisa to Italy.
   b. An Italian museum refuses to allow a Leonardo da Vinci exhibition to go to France.
   c. France believes that Leonardo da Vinci was French, and Italy disagrees.
   d. There aren't enough Leonardo da Vinci works to go around.

2. Leonardo da Vinci is important for many reasons. Which of the following is <u>not</u> one of those reasons?
   a. He supported Italian nationalism.
   b. He was a skilful painter.
   c. He is an important symbol of the Renaissance.
   d. He conceived many great projects.

3. When was Leonardo da Vinci born?
   a. less than 400 years ago
   b. less than 500 years ago
   c. more than 500 years ago
   d. more than 600 years ago

▍What do you remember?

4. According to the Uffizi Gallery, what is the problem with moving Leonardo da Vinci's paintings?

_____

5. According to the Italian woman, what allowed Leonardo da Vinci to grow into a great artist?

_____

6. Why does the French man think that Leonardo da Vinci was French?

_____

●●Background Information●●

　2019年は世界各地でルネサンスの巨匠レオナルド・ダ・ヴィンチの記念行事が企画されました。イタリア出身の彼は、フランス王家の招きに応じてフランスに居を移した後、トゥール近郊で死去しており、その縁もあってルーヴル美術館は、2019年秋に大規模なダ・ヴィンチ展の開催を計画しました。イタリアの民主党政権は2017年、ウフィツィ美術館所蔵のダ・ヴィンチ作品を、特に脆弱な作品を除いてルーヴルの求めに応じて貸与すると約束し、その見返りにフランス側は、2020年の画家ラファエロ（Raphael, 1483-1520）没後500周年に、国内のラファエロの作品をイタリアに貸与すると約束していました。しかし、ニュースにある通り、2018年11月に、イタリアの極右政党である「同盟（Lega）」所属のボルゴンツォーニ文化次官が新聞インタビューにおいて、ダ・ヴィンチの作品のフランスへの貸与を見直すと発言し、物議を醸しました。

　ボルゴンツォーニ文化次官は、協定がフランス側に一方的に有利な不平等なものであるため修正を求めると述べました。しかしこの騒動は、美術品をめぐる1つの協定に留まるものではありません。イタリアは、2018年6月に左派と右派の大衆主義2党の率いる連立政権が発足して以来、フランスとの間に緊張関係が生じています。特に、「同盟」を率いるサルビーニ内相はフランス批判の急先鋒で、事あるごとにマクロン政権を批判してきました。今回の一件には、こうした両国間の亀裂が背景にあるのです。この騒動や、対リビア政策の違いなどの様々な要因を経て、フランスは2019年2月、在伊フランス大使を呼び戻す事態となりました。結局、驚いたイタリア側が懐柔策を打ち、1週間後には大使が戻ると発表されました。この両国の諍いが、どのようにEUの内部政治に影響を及ぼすか、懸念の声が上がっています。

参考：https://www.theguardian.com/travel/2019/jan/18/10-european-art-anniversaries-in-2019-exhibitions-bauhaus-leonardo

http://trulies-europe.de/?p=611

https://qz.com/1548392/a-feud-between-france-and-italy-sums-up-the-deep-rift-over-europe/

Filling Gaps **News Story** CD2-08 [Original] CD2-09 [Voiced]

▌ Watch the News, then fill the gaps in the text.

Newsreader: Now, do you recognise this painting? The artist, of course, the original Renaissance man and the (¹   ) of Europe, but today Leonardo da Vinci has found himself at the centre of an international (²   ). James Reynolds is in Florence for us with the story.

5

James Reynolds: Take as much time as you need in front of each of these early Leonardo paintings (³   ) (⁴   ) in Florence. They will 10 not be going on tour to (⁵   ) the Mona Lisa at the Louvre in Paris.

Reynolds: You'd think that there'd be (⁶   ) Leonardo works to go around, to keep everyone happy. But that's not how this argument is playing out. The artist is now essentially the subject of an international 15 (⁷   ) dispute.

Reynolds: The Uffizi Gallery says that the works are too (⁸   ) to be moved.

Eike Schmidt, Director, the Uffizi Gallery: Any travel always puts works of art at (⁹   ). I mean, there are very, very sophisticated, er, ways of 20 having paintings, er, travel nowadays. Er, however, nothing is as safe as keeping, er, them where they are.

Reynolds: But there's much more to it than simple (¹⁰   ). Right now, populist-led Italy and liberal-run France do not (¹¹   ) (¹²   ).

25

Reynolds: Italy (¹³   ) France of trying to hijack Leonardo for itself.

Lucia Borgonzoni, Italian undersecretary for the Ministry of Cultural Heritage and Activities, member of the League party (*translated from Italian*): Leonardo as such (¹⁴   ) to the world of course, but if you ask me

30

where he is from, he's Italian. He was an Italian (^{15}). And the fact that he was (^{16}) by all this Italian beauty, this environment, allowed him to grow and become what he is now.

35

Reynolds: But France, the (^{17}) of the artist's most famous work, feels no need for history lessons from Italy.

Jack Lang, former French Culture Minister: What a (^{18})! What 40 a, what a (^{19}). Yes, Leonardo is Italian. But he has chosen, freely chosen, to come in France, and to live, er, in, er, this country during several years, and he has (^{20}) many great projects. Leonardo is Italian, but at the same time he was French, he was European.

Reynolds: A (^{21}) continent now prepares to mark the 500th 45 anniversary of Leonardo's death, the renaissance (^{22}) who once dreamed of flight is now grounded in a nationalistic debate. James Reynolds, BBC News, Florence.

(Wednesday 23 January 2019)

Notes ··

I. 1: **this painting**「この絵」レオナルド・ダ・ヴィンチの代表作『モナ・リザ』(the Mona Lisa, c. 1503-17) を指す。フランスのルーヴル美術館に所蔵されている I. 3: **Renaissance**「ルネサンス」14-16世紀に栄えた古典芸術の復興運動、ならびにその期間を指す。イタリアで始まり、ヨーロッパ中に広まった I. 5: **Leonardo da Vinci**「レオナルド・ダ・ヴィンチ (1452-1519)」ルネサンス期を代表するイタリア出身の芸術家。絵画、彫刻、建築、工学、解剖学など、様々な分野で多彩な才能を発揮した。空中飛行の実現を目指し、飛行器具を考案したことでも知られている I. 7: **Florence**「フィレンツェ」イタリア中部の都市 I. 11: **the Louvre**「ルーヴル美術館」フランスのパリにある世界最大規模の美術館。1793年開館 I. 17: **The Uffizi Gallery**「ウフィツィ美術館」フィレンツェにある美術館。ルネサンス期の作品を多数所蔵している。16世紀に設立された I. 24: **populist-led**「大衆主義者主導の」populistとは、エリート主義 (elitism) に対抗し、一般大衆を扇動し味方につけて政治活動を行う者 I. 28: **the Ministry of Cultural Heritage and Activities**「文化財・文化活動省」文化財の保護を行うイタリアの行政機関 I. 30: **League**「同盟」イタリアの右派政党。イタリア語ではLegaと呼ばれる

イギリス貴族の修学旅行、グランドツアー

17、18世紀のイギリスにおいて、裕福な貴族の子弟がヨーロッパ大陸を旅行する「グランドツアー（Grand Tour）」が流行しました。主な行き先は当時文化的な先進国であったフランスとイタリアで、フランスではフランス風の衣服を身につけて上品なマナーを学び、イタリアでは古代ローマやルネサンスの遺跡を見学することが人気でした。哲学者のトマス・ホッブズ（Thomas Hobbes, 1588-1679）や経済学者のアダム・スミス（Adam Smith, 1723-79）も家庭教師として旅行に同行したことがありました。

▶▶▶ Moving On

6 Making a Summary

▮ Fill the gaps to complete the summary.

Leonardo da Vinci is an important symbol of the Renaissance, and the (t   ) of Europe. The year 2019 is the 500th anniversary of his death. His paintings are in museums all over the world, including the Louvre, in Paris. However, there is a (s   ) between Italy and France, about which country should have (c   ) of his paintings. The Uffizi Gallery is refusing to allow a da Vinci exhibition to leave Italy, because they say the works are too (f   ) to be moved. However, there is more to it than (c   ). There is also a nationalistic debate. Italy says that Leonardo's works should stay in Italy because he was Italian. On the other hand, a French man said that although it wasn't a (r   ) that he was Italian, he was also French because he lived there and (c   ) many projects there. In fact, he was European.

7 Follow Up

▮ Discuss, write or present.

1. Do you agree that Leonardo da Vinci was so important? Spend some time finding out about him, and share what you know with other students.

2. What do you think about the Italian opinion that Leonardo da Vinci's works should stay in Italy because he was Italian? Do you think that works by Japanese artists, like Hokusai, should remain in Japan?

3. Find out about the Elgin Marbles, which are in the British Museum, and which Greece wants to be returned to Greece. The British Museum says that they are being carefully looked after because they belong to all the world, and not just to Greece. What do you think?

Unit 12

The Success of Hip and Knee Replacements

医療の進歩で長寿化が進む中、健康で活発な生活をできるだけ長く送ることは、多くの人にとっての願いです。脚や膝の痛みに苦しむ高齢者に希望をもたらしてくれるニュースを見てみましょう。

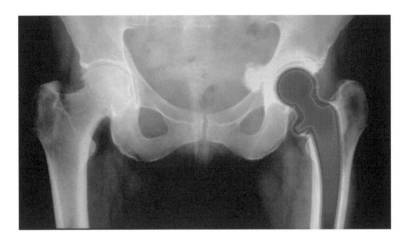

▶ Starting Off

1 Setting the Scene

▌ What do you think?

1. What happens to your body as you get older? Is there any way to stop this change?
2. It is now possible to have parts of your body replaced by artificial parts. Do you know what parts can be replaced?
3. Do you know of anybody who has had a hip or knee replacement? Why did they have it, and was it successful? Tell your partner about it.

2 Building Language

▌ For each word (1-5), find two synonyms (a-j).

1. effective [/]
2. intense [/]
3. restrict [/]
4. reassure [/]
5. accurate [/]

a. extreme   f. curb
b. useful   g. exact
c. correct   h. functional
d. impede   i. convince
e. encourage   j. acute

3 Understanding Check 1

Read the quotes, then watch the news and match them to the right people.

1. . . . patients can go into their surgery, or when deciding whether to have surgery . . .   [   ]

2. . . . a new study suggests the majority of knee and hip replacements last . . .

   [   ]

3. It was magic.   [   ]

4. . . . carries out almost 200,000 hip and knee replacements each year.

   [   ]

4 Understanding Check 2

Which is the best answer?

1. According to research, which of the following is true?
   a. Nearly 60% of hip replacements last for 25 years.
   b. Over 25% of knee replacements last for 60 years.
   c. More than 80% of hip replacements last for 25 years.
   d. Fewer than 80% of knee replacements last for 25 years.

2. Which of the following was <u>not</u> mentioned as a benefit of this research?
   a. Patients and surgeons can make more informed decisions.
   b. Patients are reassured that they can stay active.
   c. More people will be able to afford replacements.
   d. The health service can plan its resources.

3. How many years after her hip replacement will Wendy go to Barbados?
   a. ten years
   b. seventeen years
   c. twenty-five years
   d. twenty-seven years

▌What do you remember?

4. Why did Wendy have a replacement, and how did she feel afterwards?

_____

5. What are the problems in having a replacement a second time?

_____

6. Why will more people need hip and knee replacements in the future?

_____

●●Background Information●●

　股関節と膝関節は、二足歩行の人類にとって身体を支える非常に重要な位置を占め、しかも負担の大きい部分であり、軟骨や組織など、メカニズムも精巧です。関節は骨と骨の繋ぎ目にあたります。骨と骨は堅いもの同士で、直接触れ合うと磨り減ってしまいます。それを防ぐため、正常な関節部分の骨の表面は、軟骨という滑らかな層で覆われています。軟骨には神経や血管がありません。水分が多く、関節にかかる衝撃を吸収し、関節を滑らかに動かす役目があります。さらに関節部分は、関節包という袋のようなもので覆われていて、その内側にある滑膜という膜から、潤滑油の役割をする関節液が分泌されています。このようにして、痛みを感じることなく自由に関節を動かすことができるのです。

　関節の中でも、股関節と膝関節は、体重を支えながら動くという人間の基本的な動作に重要な役割を果たしています。しかし、このような精巧な仕組みゆえ、食事・運動・体重・加齢などによる様々な影響を受けやすく、故障や障害も心配されます。障害が引き起こされた時、人工関節を用いる方法がありますが、手術に踏み切るかどうか、不安を覚え、躊躇する人も多いのです。そんな中、ニュースにあるように、朗報が届きました。人工関節の寿命が、以前考えられていたより長持ちするというデータが集まったのです。

　人工関節手術にまで至らなくても、生活改善などの保存療法もあります。関節を動かすためには、その周辺にある筋肉を使いますが、関節に問題が生じて痛みが出たり関節の動きが悪くなったりすると、関節を動かさないでいることが多くなります。すると、その関節の周辺の筋力が低下してしまい、さらに関節が動きにくくなる、という悪循環を生んでしまいます。保存療法では、食事・運動・体重をコントロールすることで改善を図ります。また、骨切り手術、ヒアルロン酸注射や最先端の再生医療などもあります。患者本人から極少量の皮下脂肪を取り、幹細胞を培養する培養幹細胞治療は、痛みを大幅に軽減することができます。医学の進歩を身近に感じる話題です。

参考：https://www.health.harvard.edu/healthbeat/harvard-expert-what-you-can-expect-from-knee-and-hip-surgery
　　　https://www.thelancet.com/series/hip-and-knee-replacement
　　　https://www.ucihealth.org/blog/2017/05/hip-knee-replacement

Unit 12　*The Success of Hip and Knee Replacements*　**69**

Filling Gaps   **News Story**   CD2-11 [Original]   CD2-12 [Voiced]

Watch the News, then fill the gaps in the text.

Newsreader: Now, a new study suggests the majority of knee and hip replacements last much longer than (^{1}) thought. Researchers at the University of Bristol say replacement (^{2}) can remain (^{3}) for up to 25 years. It's hoped the findings will help doctors and patients decide when to carry out (^{4}). Here's our health correspondent, Jenny Walrond.

5

Jenny Walrond: Eighty-year-old Wendy, 17 years on from a hip replacement, cycles 10 more often than she drives.

Wendy Fryer: I was in (^{5}) pain, so it (^{6}) everything I wanted to do, even cycling was getting quite difficult. And then I had the (^{7}), and I woke up, and it was like a new person. It was magic.

Walrond: Hip and knee replacements are two of the most (^{8}) types of surgery. Until now, doctors haven't been able to give patients (^{9}) information about how long they'll continue to work. But a study (^{10}) in *The Lancet* journal shows many joint replacements last for 25 years. For knees, it's over 80%, and almost 60% of hip replacements. Much longer than previously thought.

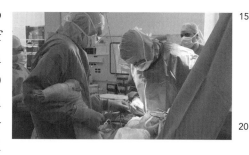

15

20

Walrond: Having surgery a second time on a replacement is more (^{11}), and less likely to be (^{12}). So knowing the 25 joints will last longer can help both patients and surgeons to make more (^{13}) (^{14}).

Dr. Jonathan Evans, Bristol Medical School: The main (^{15}) is that patients can go into their surgery, or when deciding whether to have surgery, with their eyes open. They understand exactly what the (^{16}) are,

30

and exactly how long this hip replacement, or knee replacement, is likely to last.

Walrond: The NHS in England and Wales carries out almost 200,000 hip and knee replacements each year. Knowing how long they'll last (^{17}) the health service to plan its resources, at a time when our (^{18}) (^{19}) means more people will need them.

Walrond: Today's research can (^{20}) patients like Wendy, that they too can stay (^{21}) for longer. She's hoping her hip will last at least another ten years.

Fryer: One of my grandsons wants me to take him to Barbados when I'm 90. So I've got to live till I'm 90 and take him to Barbados like he wants me to do. So, (^{22}) it will be good.

Walrond: Jenny Walrond, BBC News, Bristol.

(Friday 15 February 2019)

Notes ···

l. 4: **the University of Bristol** 「ブリストル大学」イングランド南西部の都市ブリストルにある大学 l. 21: **The Lancet** 『ランセット』週刊で発行されている国際的な医学雑誌。1823年創刊 l. 37: **The NHS (＝National Health Service)** 「国民保健サービス」国営の医療サービス l. 46: **Barbados** 「バルバドス」カリブ海にある、イギリス連邦の島国

▶▶▶ Moving On

6 Making a Summary   ◉ CD2-13

▌ **Fill the gaps to complete the summary.**

　　The National Health Service in England and Wales carries out 200,000 hip and knee replacements every year. Recent research has found that almost 60% of hip, and over 80% of knee replacements remain (e　　　　　) for 25 years, much longer than (p　　　　　　) thought. The main (i　　　　　) of this is that patients and surgeons are better informed with (a　　　　　) information, and know the risks. Also, the health service can plan its (r　　　　　), as they can avoid a second operation, which would be more expensive and less likely to succeed. And patients are (r　　　　　) that replacements will last long enough. For example, Wendy had her operation 17 years ago, because the (i　　　　) pain (r　　　　　) her activities. Now, she can ride a bicycle with ease, and is planning to go to Barbados in ten years, when she will be 90.

7 Follow Up

▌ **Discuss, write or present.**

1. Wendy is 80 years old and rides a bicycle. She wants to go to Barbados when she is 90. Do you think that you will be as active as her when you are her age? What sort of person do you hope you will be? Describe your future self.

2. Hip and knee replacement operations are expensive. Do you think that these should be paid for through the government's national insurance system, or should patients pay for them privately?

3. Research into health issues is very important. What other issues do you think we should conduct research into?

Britons Apply for German Citizenship

EU離脱の先行きが見えない中、他のEU諸国で暮らすイギリスの人々はどうしているのでしょうか。ドイツに住むイギリス人の姿を見てみましょう。

▶ Starting Off

1 Setting the Scene

▌ What do you think?

1. What do you know about Brexit? How might it affect British people who live in Europe?

2. Is your nationality important to you? In what circumstance do you think you might want to change it, or add another one?

3. Why do you think a British person might want to become a Japanese citizen?

2 Building Language

▌ Which word or phrase (1-5) best fits which explanation (a-e)?

1. citizenship   [   ]   **a.** temporarily stopped or delayed
2. constantly   [   ]   **b.** happening all the time, or again and again
3. on hold   [   ]   **c.** the status of being entitled to hold a country's passport
4. ceremonious   [   ]   **d.** difficult; requires care
5. tricky   [   ]   **e.** especially polite or formal

③ Understanding Check 1

▌ Read the quotes, then watch the news and match them to the right people.

1. I just don't know what's going to happen.   [   ]

2. Here are my two identities.   [   ]

3. . . . it's only half of the problem.   [   ]

4. . . . Germany was the place that welcomed most new citizens from the UK that year.   [   ]

④ Understanding Check 2

▌ Which is the best answer?

1. Which of the following is correct?
   a. 100,000 British people returned to the UK from Germany after the referendum, but only 6,000 were granted citizenship.
   b. At least 100,000 British people live in Germany, but since the referendum more than 6,000 have gone home.
   c. More than 100,000 British people live in Germany, and in 2017 more than 6,000 were granted citizenship.
   d. There are four times the number of British people living in Germany than any other EU country.

2. In order to become a German citizen, what are the requirements?
   a. You must have arrived at least six years ago, or less if you are married to a German, and speak German.
   b. You must have worked in Germany for six years and speak German.
   c. You must have been married to a German for six years and speak German.
   d. You must be married to a German-speaker who has lived there for six years.

3. If Britons resident in Germany want a German passport, why must they hurry?
   a. It takes a long time to get a passport, so they must apply quickly.
   b. EU citizens cannot choose dual nationality.
   c. Too many citizens will be applying for passports after Brexit.
   d. When the UK leaves the EU, Germany will not allow dual nationality.

▌What do you remember?

4. How long did it take Rachel Marriott (the first woman) to get her citizenship, and what did she do when she received it?

_____

5. Why is it hard for Rose Newell (the second woman) to become German?

_____

6. Why did Rachel Clarke (the third woman) put off applying for German citizenship?

_____

●●Background Information●●

　2016年6月23日の国民投票でEU離脱を決定したイギリスを率いたのは、史上2人目の女性首相テリーザ・メイ（Theresa May, 1956- ）でしたが、議会は混迷するまま2019年6月7日、保守党党首を辞任しました。同年7月、ボリス・ジョンソンが首相に就任し、解散総選挙の勝利を経て、2020年1月31日にいよいよEU離脱が行われました。ただし、2020年12月31日までは移行期間とされ、記念硬貨発行や新規パスポートの色が変わる程度で、市民生活に大きな変化は及ばないようです。

　1967年に発足した「ヨーロッパ共同体（EC: European Community）」が1993年に発展改称した「ヨーロッパ連合（EU: European Union）」は、1991年締結のマーストリヒト条約に基づき、加盟国のさらなる経済的・政治的統合を推進するために設立されました。その結果EU内の旅行や居住は比較的自由になり、他国に移住する人がたくさんいます。このような状況でイギリスは国民投票でEU離脱を選び、ヨーロッパの他国に住むイギリス人やイギリスに住むEU加盟国の国民に動揺が走りました。

　ニュースで取り上げられているように、ドイツ、フランス、またはイタリアに住むイギリス人の多くが、居住国の市民権を申請しました。特にドイツは、EU加盟国以外の二重国籍を認めていないため、イギリスの離脱前に市民権を申請する人が多くいました。また、オーストリア、スペイン、オランダなど、通常二重国籍を認めていない国もあり、そのような国に住むイギリス人は外国人として暮らすか、イギリスの国籍を諦めるか、苦しい選択を迫られることになりそうです。

参考：https://www.bbc.com/news/world-europe-47536982

　　　https://www.thelocal.es/20190108/brits-in-spain-hope-government-could-open-up-to-dual-citizenship-legislation-in-2019

　　　https://www.theguardian.com/politics/2019/may/05/labour-mps-say-they-wont-back-a-brexit-deal-without-a-peoples-vote

▍ **Watch the News, then fill the gaps in the text.**

Newsreader: Now, the continued (^{1} _____) surrounding Brexit means the rights of UK citizens living in EU countries are still to be (^{2} _____). Instead of waiting to see what's coming up, an increasing number of them are applying for (^{3} _____) in the European country where they live and work. The figure more than (^{4} _____) in 2017. That was the year after the Brexit referendum, and Germany was the place that welcomed most new citizens from the UK that year. Jean Mackenzie has met some of them in Berlin.

Name: Rachel Marriott
Age: 31
Occupation: Kindergarten teacher
Time in Germany: 8 years

5

10

Jean Mackenzie: Germany is home to at least 100,000 Brits, and since the referendum record numbers have applied for (^{5} _____). We followed three people as they try to (^{6} _____) their future here.

15

Rachel Marriott: When I woke up on the morning after the referendum, the bottom (^{7} _____) out of my life.

Mackenzie: She applied for (^{8} _____) almost immediately, and says the process was so stressful it made her ill.

Marriott: The wait was awful, like, it was (^{9} _____) in the back of my head.
Every time I went to the mailbox I was like, it could be there, it could be there, it could be there.

20

Mackenzie: Finally, after more than a year, the letter (^{10} _____).

Marriott: Here are my two identities.

Marriott: I just started crying like . . .

Mackenzie: Why was it so (^{11} _____)?

Name: Rose Newell
Age: 32
Occupation: Translator
Time in Germany: 6 years

25

Marriott: Because it was over.

Became a German citizen 3 weeks ago

Mackenzie: To become a German citizen, you must have lived in the country for six years and speak the language. But you can apply (^{12} _____), if you're married to a German.

30

Mackenzie: Rose and her partner Renee got married three months after the referendum. But Brexit has put their other plans (^{13}) (^{14}).

Name: Rachel Clarke
Age: 40
Occupation: Theatre Director
Time in Germany: 20 years

Waiting to find out if she's been granted citizenship

Rose Newell: We wanted to (^{15}) to the UK. Um, and that was our plan, having a house with a garden near to my mum. And now we're looking to buy it in Germany.

Newell: It wasn't particularly (^{16}).

Newell: There's a feeling of, er, being rubber-stamped and (^{17}). But I'm, it's only half of the problem. I mean my heart's still British. It would be different if I didn't care about the UK, but I do. It's hard.

Mackenzie: In 2017, the year after the referendum, Germany granted (^{18}) to more than 6,000 Brits. That's four times the (^{19}) of any other EU country.

Mackenzie: Rachel came to Germany to study and never left. But she's put off applying for a passport until three months ago.

Rachel Clarke: I never actually thought about doing that because I thought, "Come on, we're all European, I don't need to do it." And then (^{20}) I realised it was December, and I hadn't done anything about it.

Mackenzie: Because her work is (^{21}), she's been told that getting a German passport might be (^{22}).

Clarke: So, if I really did have to go home, I would have to start from (^{23}). I just don't know what's going to happen.

Mackenzie: For those hoping for a second passport, time is running out. Only EU citizens can apply for (^{24}) nationality in Germany. After Brexit, Brits will have to choose. Jean Mackenzie, BBC News.

(Tuesday 19 March 2019)

Notes ··

l. 2: **Brexit**「イギリスのEU離脱」 l. 9: **the Brexit referendum**「EU離脱を問う国民投票」2016年6月23日に行われた、イギリスのEU（欧州連合）からの離脱を決定した国民投票を指す

イギリス王室とドイツの関係

　ライバル国家として捉えられがちなイギリスとドイツですが、実は現在のイギリス王室の祖先はドイツ人です。スチュアート朝最後の君主、アン女王（Queen Anne, 1665-1714）が亡くなった後、ジョージ1世（King George I, 1660-1727）がドイツから迎えられ、ハノーヴァー朝が始まりました。ジョージ1世は英語が話せなかったため、議会に対して「英国王は君臨すれども統治せず（The English sovereign reigns, but does not rule.）」の原則が打ち立てられました。その後、ヴィクトリア女王（Queen Victoria, 1819-1901）も、ドイツからアルバート公（Prince Albert, 1819-61）を夫に迎えました。

▶▶▶ Moving On

6 Making a Summary

CD2-16

❙ Fill the gaps to complete the summary.

In a (r　　　　　　) in 2016, the UK decided to leave the European Union. This meant that the rights of UK citizens living in the EU could not be guaranteed. Therefore some of them have decided to apply for (c　　　　　　) where they live. Germany is home for 100,000 Brits, and in 2017, more than 6,000 of them became German citizens. Applicants must hurry because when Britain leaves the EU, (d　　　　　) nationality will not be possible. Rachel Marriott applied immediately, but it took a year and she worried (c　　　　　) about it. Rose Newell married a German citizen, and now she has German citizenship. It wasn't (c　　　　　) and she felt that she was just being (r　　　　　). The couple's other plans are still (o　　　　) (h　　　　), and she still cares about the UK. Rachel Clarke did not apply for a German passport until last December. She was told that it would be (t　　　　) because her work was (f　　　　　), and, in any case, she thought it shouldn't be necessary, as we are all European.

7 Follow Up

❙ Discuss, write or present.

1. The women had made Germany their home, but Brexit meant that they'd become foreigners. What choices would you make in that situation?
2. Find out what the requirements are for a foreigner to get a Japanese passport.
3. Rachel Marriott (the first woman), showed us her two passports and said "Here are my two identities". What do you think she meant? Can you behave like two different people if you have two nationalities?

Unit 14
Squirrel on the Menu

ロンドンでリス料理を提供するレストランが登場しましたが、人々の反応は様々です。リス肉は、どのような経緯を経て、供されるようになったのでしょうか。ニュースを見てみましょう。

▶ Starting Off

1 Setting the Scene

▮ What do you think?

1. What is your favourite food?
2. Is there anything that you would absolutely refuse to eat?
3. What is the strangest thing that you have ever eaten? Tell the story to your partner.

2 Building Language

▮ Which word (1-5) best fits which explanation (a-e)?

1. fluffy   [   ]   **a.** soft and light, like a toy
2. speechless [   ]   **b.** reduce the numbers of an animal by killing some of
3. cull   [   ]   them
4. decline   [   ]   **c.** throw carelessly
5. chuck   [   ]   **d.** a fall in numbers or quality
                        e. amazed; unable to describe one's feelings

3 Understanding Check 1

▌ **Read the quotes, then watch the news and match them to the right people.**

1. We're not actively going out hunting squirrels to serve to people. [   ]

2. ... causing them to now become endangered. [   ]

3. So what we have is a source of meat ... [   ]

4. I never thought I would eat squirrel. [   ]

4 Understanding Check 2

▌ **Which is the best answer?**

1. What special dish is on the menu of a London restaurant?
   a. squirrel stew
   b. squirrel on toast
   c. squirrel lasagna
   d. roast squirrel

2. Which of the following is true?
   a. Red Squirrels arrived in the UK in the 19th century.
   b. Grey squirrels have now become endangered.
   c. When grey squirrels were introduced to North America, they changed colour.
   d. After grey squirrels came to the UK, the number of red squirrels began to go down.

3. The people had different responses to eating squirrel. Which one of the following responses did we <u>not</u> hear?
   a. It's cruel to squirrels.
   b. It sounds disgusting.
   c. I want to try it.
   d. It tastes delicious.

What do you remember?

4. Why are gamekeepers culling grey squirrels?

_____

5. Why does the supermarket owner consider grey squirrel meat to be sustainable?

_____

6. Why will the government continue to control the number of grey squirrels?

_____

●●Background Information●●

　今回のニュースは、ロンドンの「ネイティヴ（Native）」というレストランで、ハイイロリス（grey squirrel）の肉を使ったメニューが提供されたという話題でした。

　なぜハイイロリスが食肉にされることになったのでしょうか。イギリス在来種のリスはアカリス（red squirrel）で、スコットランド、カンブリア、ノーサンブリア、ワイト島、プール・ハーバーの島々に、約16万匹が生息しています。一方、19世紀にアメリカから持ち込まれたハイイロリスは、約200万匹にまで増加しています。その原因は、ハイイロリスがアカリスを生息地から追い出したり、アカリスにとって致命的なリス痘（squirrel pox）というウイルスを伝染させたりすることにあります。また、2005年には、グロスターシャーのディーンの森で、ハイイロリスの数が10万匹にまで増え、木の皮を剥いで木を枯らしてしまうことが問題になりました。

　このような理由で、イギリスではハイイロリスの数を抑制することが長年の課題になっています。1930年代初めに最初の取り組みが行われ、1940年代には「ハイイロリス射撃クラブ（grey squirrel shooting clubs）」が多数結成されました。これらの団体には、当局によって猟銃の弾薬が無料で配布され、ハイイロリス1匹につき2シリングの報奨金が与えられました。現在、ハイイロリスの数を抑制するために、捕獲、毒殺、避妊などが行われていますが、抗凝血性ワルファリンという殺鼠剤を用いた毒殺は誤ってアカリスを殺す危険性があり、経口薬による避妊は一時的な効果しかありません。ブリストル大学の研究によると、ハイイロリスを殺すことは、アカリスの保護に有効ではなく、代わりに針葉樹の森を増やしたり、アカリスを島に隔離したりする方が現実的な解決策であると言います。

　動物愛護団体による否定的な意見がある一方、ハイイロリスの肉は人気を集めつつあります。2006年には、「アカリス保護パートナーシップ（the Red Squirrel Protection Partnership）」という団体が設立され、900人のボランティアと共に、2009年5月までに約22,000匹のハイイロリスを捕獲しました。それらのリスはレストランや肉屋に提供され、需要に供給が追い付かない状況です。

参考：https://www.bbc.com/news/uk-scotland-edinburgh-east-fife-12989019
　　　https://www.bbc.com/news/uk-england-gloucestershire-29443240

❚ Watch the News, then fill the gaps in the text.

Newsreader: You'll be (^{1}) with the grey squirrel as a (^{2}) (^{3}) to your garden, but would you consider eating them? Well, that's exactly what (^{4}) at one London restaurant are doing, where squirrel lasagna is now on the menu. It's not to everyone's taste though, as Linzi Kinghorn has been finding out.   5

Linzi Kinghorn: Grey squirrels. Some will admire their cute (^{5}) tails, but for others it's a tasty dish.   10

First woman: I think it's a (^{6}) meat. It tastes delicious. Why not?

First man: I never thought I would eat squirrel. But it's delicious. It's light and I'm, um, um, (^{7}).

Kinghorn: Tasty for some, but perhaps shocking for others. One London restaurant says it has its reasons for using the meat to cook with.   15

Ivan Tisdall-Downes, Head Chef, Native: We're not actively going out hunting squirrels to serve to people. It's, it is effectively a (^{8}) (^{9}). So the, er, the gamekeepers, er, are (^{10}) the squirrels because the squirrels go and eat the, the baby bird eggs, um, or they destroy the, er, the trees. The squirrels come in and rip the bark off and then 20 destroy them unfortunately. Um, so these guys are (^{11}) all the squirrels. Then the meat's going to waste.

Kinghorn: Grey squirrels were first introduced into London and the UK in the 19th century from North America. But since their arrival, the numbers of the UK's native squirrel, the red squirrel, have been in (^{12}), causing 25 them to now become endangered. And this is one of the reasons why they're now being (^{13}) and a leading supermarket has chosen to sell it.

Andrew Thornton, owner of Thornton's Budgens: They were just being (^{14}) into landfill. So what 30

we have is a source of meat that is very
(^{15}) because   they're,
they're wild, and they would be kind of   35
thrown away otherwise.

Kinghorn: Despite these reasons, this is not a
(^{16}) (^{17}) for
everyone.

Kinghorn: How do you feel about eating squirrel?   40

Second woman: No.

Third woman: I would say no. Er, I don't know what it tastes like but it just . . .

Second woman: No, it sounds disgusting.

Third woman: Yeah, it sounds disgusting, yeah.

Second man: No, that's not something. Um, no. They're too (^{18}) 45
animals for me to eat them on the (^{19}).

Third man: What? Ha, ha, ha. I don't know.

Fourth man: I'd try it.

Fifth man: I'd rather not try.

Sixth man: I'll try. Yeah.   50

Kinghorn: The government says it will continue to (^{20}) the number
of grey squirrels in order to (^{21}) other endangered (^{22}).
Linzi Kinghorn, BBC London News.

(Friday 8 February 2019)

Notes ···

l. 16: **Native** 「ネイティヴ」ロンドンのサザーク地区にある、猟鳥・猟獣の肉を中心に出しているレストラン
l. 30: **Thornton's Budgens** 「ソーントンズ・バジェンズ」Unit 3でも取り上げられているイギリスのスーパーマーケット。同スーパーでは2010年からハイイロリス肉の販売を始め、2019年時点で1パック（約200グラム）が3.84ポンド（約540円）で売られている

イギリスのジビエ

　近年日本で注目されているジビエ（gibier）とは、食用にするために狩猟によって捕獲された野生動物や野鳥を指すフランス語です。英語ではgameと言い、かつて野生で入手され、現在家畜として生産されるようになった動物の肉も含みます。代表的なジビエにはウズラやシカなどがありますが、ウサギ肉もイギリス人にとってはおなじみの食材で、パイやシチューの材料として用いられます。日本でも人気のビアトリクス・ポター（Beatrix Potter, 1866-1947）の絵本『ピータラビットのお話』（*The Tale of Peter Rabbit*, 1902）にも、ウサギのピーターのお父さんが農家の人間に捕らえられ、パイにされてしまったという記述があります。ウサギと同様、今後はリスの肉も定番の食材になっていくのかどうか、注目されるところです。

▶▶▶ Moving On

6 Making a Summary

 CD2-19

▌ Fill the gaps to complete the summary.

　　Grey squirrels are cute wild animals with (f　　　　) tails, which were introduced to the UK in the 19th century. Unfortunately, they eat baby birds' eggs, destroy trees, and have been causing a (d　　　　　) in the number of (n　　　　　) red squirrels. This is why gamekeepers have been (c　　　　　) grey squirrels. Recently, a London restaurant has put squirrel lasagna on its menu. They say it is (s　　　　　　) meat, because otherwise it would just be (c　　　　) into landfill and go to waste. Some people find the idea of eating squirrels (d　　　　　), but others would like to try it. One person found it to be so delicious that he was (s　　　　　　).

7 Follow Up

▌ Discuss, write or present.

1. How do you feel about eating squirrel? Would you like to try it?
2. One reason why grey squirrels are being culled is that they are causing a serious decline in native red squirrels. What do you think of this policy? Is it right to kill one species in order to save another? Do some research and find other examples in the world where introduced species have caused damage.
3. The restaurant chef considered squirrel meat to be sustainable because otherwise it would be thrown away. Can you think of any other examples (not just meat), where we could eat something that is often just thrown away?

Climate Change Protests

世界中のティーンエイジャーが、学校を欠席して環境デモに参加しています。彼らの主張はどのようなものでしょうか。イギリスの若者の活動を見てみましょう。

▶ Starting Off

1 Setting the Scene

▌ What do you think?

1. What do you know about climate change? Are you worried about it?
2. Do you know what governments are doing to slow down climate change? Do you think their actions are enough?
3. What can we do to solve the problem of climate change, as individuals?

2 Building Language

▌ Which word (1-5) best fits which explanation (a-e)?

1.	inspire	[ ]	**a.**	constant change or variation; instability
2.	proactive	[ ]	**b.**	give hope; have an encouraging influence
3.	fluctuation	[ ]	**c.**	include as a part of the whole
4.	abstain	[ ]	**d.**	refuse something because you don't want to do it
5.	incorporate	[ ]	**e.**	initiating change yourself; not waiting for others to take action

③ Understanding Check 1

▌ Read the quotes, then watch the news and match them to the right people.

1. And my children won't even get to see the Earth as it is. [ ]

2. Children and young people in the region today missed lessons ... [ ]

3. The UK Student Climate Network has four key demands of the government. [ ]

4. It might not necessarily change everything, but it's a possibility. [ ]

④ Understanding Check 2

▌ Which is the best answer?

1. All of the following are climate change issues, but which one was <u>not</u> mentioned?
   a. the loss of ice at the North Pole
   b. deforestation
   c. flooding
   d. plastic pollution

2. We often hear the following arguments, but which one was <u>not</u> made by these students?
   a. Nobody seems to be doing anything about climate change.
   b. If climate change is damaging our future so much, why must we go to school?
   c. We must elect politicians who believe that climate change is a serious problem.
   d. If we want to save ourselves, we mustn't burn any more coal.

3. Which one of the following was a demand made by UK students?
   a. The voting age should be reduced to 18.
   b. We must tell the public about the severity of the economic crisis.
   c. A state of climate emergency should be declared.
   d. National government must be reformed.

▌ What do you remember?

4. Where did these protests take place, and what country did their inspiration come from?

_____

5. According to Becky Barr, what do scientists believe?

_____

6. Why does Becky Barr think that we will hear from the young people again?

_____

●●Background Information●●

　スウェーデンが史上最も熱い夏を記録した2018年8月のある日、当時15歳だったグレタ・トゥーンベリ（Greta Thunberg, 2003- ）は、学校を休んで国会前へ行き、一人で抗議活動を始めました。以後彼女は毎週金曜日に学校を休み、抗議活動を行なっていますが、一人ではありません。口先の協定ばかりで実質的な対策を講じない指導者やメディアへの抗議活動はヨーロッパ中へ、更には世界中に広がりました。イギリスでは、2018年12月にデモに参加した4人の学生が「イギリス学生気候ネットワーク」（UKSCN: UK Students Climate Network）を立ち上げ、ニュースにあるように2019年2月15日を全国行動の日として、第1回のストライキを行いました。

　国連開発計画（UNDP: United Nations Development Programme）は、1965年の第20回国連総会決議に基づき1966年1月1日に発足し、貧困削減、民主的ガバナンスの確立、エネルギーと環境、危機予防と復興、情報通信技術及びHIV/AIDSの6分野に重点を置いて活動を行っています。2016年1月から始まった17の「持続可能な開発目標」（SDGs: Sustainable Development Goals）、通称「グローバル・ゴールズ」では、貧困に終止符を打ち、地球を保護し、すべての人が平和と豊かさを享受できるようにすることを目指すための普遍的な行動を呼びかけており、気候変動や持続可能な消費などを、新たな分野を優先課題として盛り込んでいます。こうした地球を守ることの目標の実現に向けて各国政府の対策は不十分です。それらを実現するため、若者たちが立ち上がったのです。

参考：https://www.theguardian.com/science/2018/sep/01/swedish-15-year-old-cutting-class-to-fight-the-climate-crisis
　　　https://www.theguardian.com/science/2018/sep/01/swedish-15-year-old-cutting-class-to-fight-the-climate-crisis
　　　https://www.undp.org/content/undp/en/home/sustainable-development-goals.html

5 Filling Gaps — News Story

❚ Watch the news, then fill the gaps in the text.

Male newsreader: Now, (¹   ) over climate change were held today by young people in Manchester, Preston, Liverpool and Lancaster. They've been (²   ) by a Swedish teenager, who (³   ) her country's government of not following the Paris Climate Agreement.

Female newsreader: Children and young people in the region today missed 5 lessons to hold their own protest, as Becky Barr reports.

First student (*chanting*): What do we want?

Others (*chanting*): Climate justice!

First student (*chanting*): When do we want it?

Others (*chanting*): Now!

Students (*chanting*): Save the nation! Stop (⁴   )!   10

Second student (*chanting*): What do we want?

Others (*chanting*): Climate action!

Second student (*chanting*): When do we want it?   15

Others (*chanting*): Now!

Becky Barr: In Liverpool, Lancaster and Manchester, schoolchildren and students today sought to draw (⁵   ) to the impact of climate change.

Students (*chanting*): Save our souls, don't burn coal!

Barr: As part of a national day of action, the protests saw young people walk out of 20 lessons and make their voices heard.

Third student: We're here supporting the national day of action across 30 universities and towns, and (⁶   ) the, the government to take action because they're just so laissez-faire about it.   25

Fourth student: If we don't take care of our (⁷   ), I won't get to see the Earth in like ten years. And my children won't even get to see the Earth as it is.

And it's such a beautiful planet. We need to take care of it.

Fifth student: As we get older, the Earth and climate change are just going to get worse, so we want to be (^{8}), to stop it.

Sixth student: We need everyone to really write to their MPs, let them know that this is a real issue that, er, needs to be (^{9}).

Barr: (^{10}) weather, from flooding to fire continues to grab the headlines. Scientists believe natural (^{11}) in our climate are being overtaken by a rapid human-induced warming that has serious (^{12}) for our planet. And these young people think a school strike can encourage change.

Seventh student: Well, what's the point in studying for an education for a future that might not exist?

Eighth student: When people actually (^{13}) from school, and make their way out to Liverpool from all around Merseyside, I think that gives more of an impact.

Ninth student: For them to turn around and say that learning about how to find out the area of a circle, and over things like that is more important than our future, I think, is quite wrong.

Demonstrators (*chanting*): No more (^{14})!

Barr: The UK Student Climate Network has four key demands of the government. Firstly, to (^{15}) a state of climate emergency; to reform the national curriculum; to communicate the (^{16}) of the ecological crisis with the general public; and to (^{17}) the views of young people into policymaking, and bring down the (^{18}) (^{19}) to 16.

Tenth student: I think climate change is one of our number one (^{20}) on this Earth and nobody seems to be doing any major things about it.

Eleventh student: I'm as worried about the (^{21}) (^{22}) because, um, it, it's in, a, the majority of the ocean and so many animals are being killed by it.

Twelfth student: We're hoping that it changes some people's minds about what they're doing. It might not necessarily change everything, but it's a possibility.　　　　　　　　　65

Barr: With further strikes (²³　　　　　　　),

this won't be the last we hear from these young people. Becky Barr, *BBC* 70 *North West Tonight*.

(Friday 15 February 2019)

Notes ···

l. 2: **Manchester**「マンチェスター」イングランド北西部大マンチェスターにある都市　l. 2: **Preston**「プレストン」イングランド北西部ランカシャーにある都市　l. 2: **Liverpool**「リバプール」イングランド北西部マージーサイドにある都市　l. 2: **Lancaster**「ランカスター」イングランド北西部ランカシャーにある都市　l. 3: **a Swedish teenager**「スウェーデン人のとある10代の若者」グレタ・トゥーンベリを指す〈p. 87参照〉 l. 4: **the Paris Climate Agreement**「気候変動に関するパリ協定」2020年以降の地球温暖化対策に関する枠組みを取り決めた国際協定。2015年12月12日に採択された　l. 8: **Climate justice**「気候正義」地球温暖化対策に関する不平等を正そうという思想。これまでエネルギーを大量消費してきた先進国やそれを担ってきた世代の人々が率先して責任を果たし、途上国や今後将来を担う若者世代が不利益を被らないようにすべきという主張　l. 14: **Climate action**「気候行動」気候変動への対策を行うこと　l. 24: **laissez-faire**「自由放任主義の」フランス語で「なすに任せよ」を意味する　l. 52: **The UK Student Climate Network**「イギリス学生気候ネットワーク」政府の気候変動対策に抗議すべく結成されたイギリスの18歳以下の学生のネットワーク　l. 70: ***BBC North West Tonight***『BBCノース・ウェスト・トゥナイト』BBCノース・ウェストが夜に放送しているニュース番組

エコロジーの語源

　「生態学（ecology）」という単語は、1886年にドイツの生物学者E. H. ヘッケル（E. H. Haeckel, 1834-1919）が手紙の中で使用したのが最初だとされます。ギリシア語で「家」を意味するoikosとドイツ語で「学説」を意味する-logieを合わせた造語で、自然界の生物の生存のための活動を家政機関oikosにたとえて、これを成立させる理論を究明する学問をÖkologieと呼びました。ちなみに「経済学（economy）」も語源は同じで、oikosとギリシア語で「法」を表す-nomiaが結びついてできた単語です。

▶▶▶ Moving On

6 Making a Summary

Fill the gaps to complete the summary.

　　Scientists believe that climate changes are not natural (f　　　　　), but are human-(i　　　　　), with serious (i　　　　　　) for our planet. (I　　　　　) by a Swedish teenager who accused her government of not following the Paris Climate Agreement, young people in four northern English cities have taken part in protests. They (a　　　　) from school because they felt that stopping climate change was more important for their future. They felt they had to be (p　　　　) because the government was being too laissez-faire about it, and shouted that they wanted immediate action, such as a halt to deforestation and burning coal. They have four (k　　　) demands. The government must: declare a state of emergency; reform the national curriculum; inform the public about the ecological crisis; and (i　　　　　　) young people into policymaking. They want to change people's minds, and more strikes are planned.

7 Follow Up

Discuss, write or present.

1. The students said they wanted to change peoples' minds about climate change. Did they change your mind? Do you think that their protests are effective?

2. What protests have taken place in Japan about climate change? Is the government paying attention to them? Should there be more protests, or can you trust the government to do the right thing?

3. What do you think about the students' complaint that there is no point in studying for a future that might not exist?

このテキストのメインページ
www.kinsei-do.co.jp/plusmedia/409
次のページの QR コードを読み取ると
直接ページにジャンプできます

オンライン映像配信サービス「plus⁺Media」について

本テキストの映像は plus⁺Media ページ（www.kinsei-do.co.jp/plusmedia）から、ストリーミング再生でご利用いただけます。手順は以下に従ってください。

ログイン

ログインページ

● ご利用には、ログインが必要です。
サイトのログインページ（www.kinsei-do.co.jp/plusmedia/login）へ行き、plus⁺Media パスワード（次のページのシールをはがしたあとに印字されている数字とアルファベット）を入力します。

● パスワードは各テキストにつき1つです。
有効期限は、<u>はじめてログインした時点から1年間</u>になります。

[利用方法]

次のページにある QR コード、もしくは plus⁺Media トップページ（www.kinsei-do.co.jp/plusmedia）から該当するテキストを選んで、そのテキストのメインページにジャンプしてください。

メニューページ　　　再生画面

plus+Media トップ　　　メインページ

「Video」「Audio」をタッチすると、それぞれのメニューページにジャンプしますので、そこから該当する項目を選べば、ストリーミングが開始されます。

[推奨環境]

iOS (iPhone, iPad)	OS: iOS 6 ～ 13 ブラウザ：標準ブラウザ	Android	OS: Android 4.x ～ 9.0 ブラウザ：標準ブラウザ、Chrome
PC	OS: Windows 7/8/8.1/10, MacOS X　ブラウザ：Internet Explorer 10/11, Microsoft Edge, Firefox 48以降, Chrome 53以降, Safari		

※最新の推奨環境についてはウェブサイトをご確認ください。
※上記の推奨環境を満たしている場合でも、機種によってはご利用いただけない場合もあります。また、推奨環境は技術動向等により変更される場合があります。予めご了承ください。

4097

このシールをはがすと
plus⁺Media 利用のための
パスワードが
記載されています。

一度はがすと元に戻すことは
できませんのでご注意下さい。

◀ここからはがして下さい

4097
British News Update 2

plus⁺Media

本書にはCD（別売）があります

British News Update 2
映像で学ぶ　イギリス公共放送の最新ニュース2

2020年1月20日　初版第1刷発行
2022年9月15日　初版第4刷発行

編著者　Timothy Knowles
　　　　田 村 真 弓
　　　　田 中 みんね
　　　　中 村 美帆子

発行者　福 岡 正 人
発行所　株式会社　金 星 堂
（〒101-0051）東京都千代田区神田神保町 3-21
Tel. (03)3263-3828（営業部）
　　(03)3263-3997（編集部）
Fax (03)3263-0716
http://www.kinsei-do.co.jp

編集担当　長島吉成　　　　　　　　Printed in Japan
印刷所・製本所／三美印刷株式会社

ISBN978-4-7647-4097-6 C1082